TRUE LOVE LIES

Other Works by Brad Fraser:

Love and Human Remains
Cold Meat Party
Martin Yesterday
Poor Super Man
Snake in Fridge
The Ugly Man
The Wolf Plays

True Love Lies
BRAD FRASER

PLAYWRIGHTS CANADA PRESS
TORONTO

PLAYWRIGHTS CANADA PRESS
The Canadian Drama Publisher
215 Spadina Ave., Suite 230, Toronto, ON Canada M5T 2C7
phone 416.703.0013   fax 416.408.3402
orders@playwrightscanada.com • www.playwrightscanada.com

For professional or amateur production rights, please contact
Rena Zimmerman, Great North Artists Management
350 Dupont Street
Toronto, Ontario
M5R 1V9
416.925.2051

The publisher acknowledges the support of the Canadian taxpayers through the
Government of Canada Book Publishing Industry Development Program, the Canada
Council for the Arts, the Ontario Arts Council, and the Ontario Media Development
Corporation.

Cover art and design by DC Hillier
Cover photo by Brad Fraser
Type design by Blake Sproule

LIBRARY AND ARCHIVES CANADA CATALOGUING IN PUBLICATION

Fraser, Brad, 1959-
True love lies / Brad Fraser.

Play.
ISBN 978-0-88754-915-1

I. Title.

PS8561.R294T78 2010   C812'.54   C2010-901154-6

First edition: March 2010
Printed and bound in Canada by Gauvin Press, Gatineau

For Jeff, Chad and Trevor

PLAYWRIGHT/DIRECTOR'S NOTES

It's amazing where plays come from. One minute you're working on a successful cable series and the next you're being contacted by an ex-lover you haven't seen in twenty years. A couple of emails and telephone calls later you find out he's married and has children. This leads to a few "what if?" scenarios that suddenly start to spill out onto the computer screen in a manner I'd neither foreseen nor intended until that real life incident is transformed into a highly fictional piece of dramatic fiction.

The first draft of this play came to me relatively easily. Most people liked it but I had this nagging feeling it wasn't quite what it was meant to be. So I sought out the naysayers, the people who didn't like the script, and tried to get them to talk. This is much harder than it would appear. Saying you like something is very easy, trying to pin down and explain to someone what you don't like about their work takes real effort, and many, quite rightly, can't be bothered. Fortunately there were a few who took the time and, whether or not I agreed with them, their comments helped me to peer into the play and the characters more deeply, to ask even more "what if" kinds of questions. And after a draft or two I realized the focus was wrong. I was writing another David McMillan play (*Wolfboy*, *Love and Human Remains*, *Poor Super Man*) with him as the centre point when what I really wanted to be writing was a play about the family that David just happened to appear in.

This revelation led to further rewrites and a play that maintained much of the action of the earlier draft but had that action unfold with a much different focus. Within a couple of drafts the whole play was reinvented. The people I sent it out to responded favourably and a production was set to open at my artistic home, Manchester, England's Royal Exchange Theatre, in 2009. That production, directed by Braham Murray, was a genuine hit and currently there are plans to move it into London's West End if a suitable "star" is ever found. (Don't blame me for the vagaries of the English theatrical star system.) Meanwhile a number of other productions are slated to open at various cities across North America in the coming years.

As for directing, it's been nine years since I directed for the theatre. I have done a great deal of it throughout my career but I find it very taxing. My general rule is never to direct the first production of my own play, allow some other director to premiere it and then stage the second production myself—allowing me to avoid all of the first director's pitfalls while also stealing his or her best ideas. Unfortunately that wasn't the case with this show. A sudden need for spinal surgery meant that I was only able to attend the first ten days of rehearsal in Manchester, in order to ensure the script was performable, before flying back to Canada to go under the knife. This was frustrating but, in the end, turned out to be quite liberating as well. Not having seen the RX production that Braham Murray staged means I might be in danger of repeating some of his mistakes but it also ensures that all of my work is entirely original.

Over the last few years I have become obsessed with finding ways to keep theatre in the present tense. Far too much of our stage work is obsessed with the past, relies on events from the past and is told almost entirely, often including the delivery of the performances by the actors, in that safe, slightly sentimental "past tense" style that keeps everything from being immediate. To my mind this is a betrayal of all that is unique about the theatre as an art form—which is all about its immediacy. Attempting to do this hasn't been easy. Nearly everything about the contemporary theatre has a slightly dated, museum-like quality about it and the way our writers, actors, directors, designers, etc. are trained almost invariably leads to this style of playing. However, if we manage to replace this past tense with a sense of the present, and even the future, we might just find the way plays are truly meant to be performed. Will I succeed in doing this with four weeks of rehearsal? Hard to say. But I will admit it's been a hell of a lot of fun to try.

—Brad Fraser, September 17, 2009

True Love Lies was first produced by the Royal Exchange Theatre, Manchester, England, on January 28, 2009, with the following cast and crew:

Jonny Phillips	David
John Kirk	Kane
Teresa Banham	Carolyn
Amy Beth Hayes	Madison
Oliver Gomm	Royce

Directed by Braham Murray
Set and costume design by Johanna Bryant
Lighting design by Richard Owen
Sound design by Steve Brown

True Love Lies had its North American premiere at the Factory Theatre, Toronto, on October 1, 2009, with the following cast and crew:

David Keeley	David
Ashley Wright	Kane
Julie Stewart	Carolyn
Susanna Fournier	Madison
Andrew Craig	Royce

Directed by Brad Fraser
Set and lighting design by Bretta Gerecke
Costume design by Ina Kerklaan
Sound design by Christopher Stanton
Stage managed by Sherry Roher
Apprentice stage management by Natalie Gisele
Assistant direction by Briana Brown

TRUE LOVE LIES

CHARACTERS
DAVID 50
KANE 45
CAROLYN 44
MADISON 20
ROYCE 17

SETTING
Various locales as specified. The set should not
be naturalistic. Elements should be shared by
all locations and all transitions should be made
without blackouts.

PUNCTUATION NOTE
A period is used to indicate the end of vocalization,
not necessarily the end of a thought, likewise
with capital letters at the beginning of sentences.
Commas and other punctuation have been
intentionally omitted.

ACT ONE

Lights rise on the Sawatsky kitchen. CAROLYN *is filling the dishwasher with items from the sink.* MADISON *enters.*

MADISON   Hey.

CAROLYN   Back already?

MADISON   I need to change my top.

CAROLYN   Why?

MADISON   The last place was über casual. This one's a little more classic.

CAROLYN   Who knew looking for a job was so complicated?

MADISON   Adulthood involves way too many different outfits.

MADISON exits. KANE enters.

KANE   Hello.

CAROLYN   You're early.

KANE   We're celebrating.

CAROLYN   What's the occasion?

They kiss quickly. He gives her a squeeze.

KANE   The Liebowskis loved everything about our design and I was able to get a big fat cheque out of them. I think we can now replace the furnace.

CAROLYN   I told you that design was brilliant.

KANE   They loved the chenille. Perfect choice again.

They kiss again, more passionately.

When are the kids expected?

CAROLYN   Maddy's upstairs right now.

KANE   So no time for a quick bit of.

CAROLYN   None.

KANE   Damn.

CAROLYN   Later.

KANE   Promise.

They kiss again. MADISON *enters changed.*

MADISON   Hey Pop.

KANE   How's the job hunting?

MADISON   There's not a lot out there.

CAROLYN   A job wouldn't be an issue if you were in university.

MADISON   What's the point of paying for an education if you don't know what you want to do?

          ROYCE enters.

ROYCE   Howdy.

KANE   Hey Royce. Anything cool happen today?

ROYCE   Yeah. High school's just full of cool things that happen. When's dinner?

CAROLYN   About an hour.

ROYCE   Call me.

          ROYCE exits.

MADISON   I need the car.

CAROLYN   Why?

MADISON   There's a new restaurant looking for servers and I'm already late.

CAROLYN   Do you really think working in a restaurant is going to be that much more interesting than working in a store?

MADISON   Are you kidding? Kara's working at the Poplars and you should see the money she's making. After five or six hours a night.

CAROLYN   But those late night shifts.

MADISON   Work for me.

          KANE throws MADISON his keys.

KANE   Here you go.

CAROLYN   Don't speed.

MADISON   Back in a flash.

                    MADISON exits.

CAROLYN   Let's hope this one pans out.

KANE   It's not easy getting a full-time job.

CAROLYN   Sweetie—she's twenty-one years old. She can't sell lip gloss at a kiosk three nights a week anymore.

KANE   It's still very young.

CAROLYN   Are you forgetting some of the things you'd done at that age?

KANE   They're our babies.

                    CAROLYN takes him in her arms.

CAROLYN   I like to think we didn't raise the kind of kids who live at home until they're thirty.

KANE   Would that be so bad?

CAROLYN   Yes it would.

                    A light on DAVID at the restaurant, seated at one of the tables doing paperwork. MADISON enters.

MADISON   Hi.

DAVID   Hello.

MADISON   You need waiters?

DAVID   Yes.

MADISON   I'm Madison.

DAVID   Hi Madison. David McMillan. Have we met before?

MADISON   I don't think so.

DAVID   You seem familiar.

            MADISON hands him her resumé.

MADISON   Okay. I brought my resumé.

DAVID   Do you have restaurant experience?

MADISON   No but I've got a lot of retail. Part-time.

DAVID   We're really looking for experienced waiters. I'd have to start you as a bus-person or on the coat check.

MADISON   That's fine.

DAVID   Sawatsky?

MADISON   Yes.

DAVID   You're not related to Kane Sawatsky are you?

MADISON   He's my dad. You know him?

DAVID   No not a bit a long time ago.

MADISON   Cool. Should I say hi for you?

DAVID   If you like. In all honesty Madison we are looking for people with experience in the business.

MADISON   I'm a very quick learner.

DAVID   I'm sure you are.

MADISON   I'm happy to bus or whatever.

DAVID   I'm afraid all the positions have been filled. Thanks for stopping by.

MADISON   Okay. Bye. Thanks.

               *MADISON exits. Lights rise on the Sawatsky kitchen.
               ROYCE is at the table. KANE and CAROLYN are making
               dinner.*

KANE   Did you look at those fabric samples I left on your desk?

CAROLYN   The pumpkin's too garish and that tweed stuff is an
               interesting colour but too itchy looking.

KANE   What about the aubergine?

CAROLYN   Loved the aubergine.

KANE   Whadaya wanna bet that Liebowski job leads to some
               big-time referrals?

CAROLYN   That's what we're hoping for.

ROYCE   Are those the west-end Liebowskis whose daughter
               joined that sperm cult?

KANE   I have no idea.

CAROLYN   Sperm cult?

ROYCE   Self-explanatory Ma.

               MADISON enters.

KANE   Just in time.

MADISON   I'm not hungry.

CAROLYN   What's wrong?

KANE   Did the interview go that badly?

MADISON   I got stiffed because the guy knows you.

CAROLYN   Really?

MADISON   Yeah he seemed all interested until he found out you're
             my dad.

KANE   What's his name?

MADISON   McMillan.

CAROLYN   David?

KANE   David McMillan?

MADISON   That's right. Good shape. Nice hair. A bit you know.

                     Long pause.

             What?

CAROLYN   Kane the sauce is burning.

KANE   Shit sorry damn.

CAROLYN   Everything's ready.

ROYCE   Why are you acting weird?

KANE   Madison sit.

CAROLYN   Is the sauce?

KANE   Yes. You?

CAROLYN   Yes. Go.

KANE   Hot stuff.

CAROLYN   Careful.

KANE   Sweet and sour pork chops.

CAROLYN   Grilled okra.

MADISON   Uh—guys.

KANE   Just.

CAROLYN   Eat.

MADISON   Who is David McMillan?

KANE   He was.

CAROLYN   Just a.

KANE   Friend.

CAROLYN   Of your father's.

KANE   A long time ago.

ROYCE   What kinda friend?

KANE   Just you know a friend like you have.

CAROLYN   When you have friends.

KANE   Yeah.

MADISON   So why'd he blow me off then?

KANE   We—aren't close anymore.

MADISON   Why not?

KANE   We just.

CAROLYN   Grew apart.

ROYCE   Was he a good friend?

KANE   At one time.

CAROLYN   No more talking. Eat.

              They eat. Pause.

MADISON   He seemed gay.

              Pause.

              Is he?

CAROLYN   Yes.

ROYCE   You had a gay friend?

KANE   Yes.

MADISON   So was he like your boyfriend or something? Is that why everyone's acting so weird?

              Long pause.

              Omigod.

ROYCE   Get out.

CAROLYN   It's ancient history.

MADISON   Are you kidding?

ROYCE   You're a fudgepacker?

KANE   I'm not sure we should use the term fudgepacker.

MADISON   Are you more comfortable with queer?

KANE   I don't think this is.

CAROLYN   Something we need to.

KANE   Discuss.

CAROLYN   Right now.

ROYCE   You had a boyfriend?

KANE   I he we had a relationship.

ROYCE   Relationship?

MADISON   Did you live with him?

KANE   For two years.

MADISON   Wow.

ROYCE   And you're telling us now because?

KANE   You asked.

                       Long pause.

               We can talk about it if you're.

MADISON   I'm outa here.

CAROLYN   You haven't eaten a thing.

MADISON   I said I wasn't hungry.

KANE   Any time you want. We can talk.

MADISON   Great. Thanks.

CAROLYN   Where are you going?

MADISON   Armand's.

CAROLYN   Who's Armand?

MADISON   My friend.

CAROLYN   Are you sure you wouldn't rather?

MADISON	What? Talk about the man Dad used to live with?
KANE	If you want.
MADISON	Later.

MADISON exits.

CAROLYN	We've all done things in our pasts that we're ashamed of.
KANE	Young people are supposed to try different things.
ROYCE	Like packing fudge.
KANE	Stop saying that. I just.
ROYCE	What?
KANE	It was a first-time thing.
ROYCE	It isn't bad enough having a father who's artistic and tasteful—but he turns out to be gay too.
KANE	One relationship with a man doesn't make me gay.
ROYCE	What does it make you then?
CAROLYN	Complicated. Being an adult's complicated.
ROYCE	If you say so.
KANE	We always taught you that life was about making choices. That there's nothing wrong with being different.
ROYCE	And now I get why.
KANE	Are you angry?
ROYCE	No.

CAROLYN   Where are you going?

ROYCE   To a fag bar to meet a child molester.

            ROYCE exits.

CAROLYN   He's angry.

KANE   Should we have lied?

CAROLYN   They can always tell.

KANE   And they would've heard it from someone else. Eventually.

CAROLYN   I think we should've lied.

KANE   I think you're right.

            A light on DAVID at his desk. He's reviewing resumés as he speaks on his cellphone earpiece.

DAVID   I didn't tell anyone I was selling my condo. I didn't want to be talked out of it. The fact that I've been gone for nearly five months and you just noticed should be explanation enough. Don't take it so personally. Yes. I promise Clive. Everything. I'll email you.

            Lights rise on KANE, outside of the house, smoking and pacing. MADISON enters.

MADISON   Dad.

KANE   Hey. How's Armand?

MADISON   Controlled by television. Are you smoking?

            He stubs the cigarette out quickly.

KANE   No yeah I'm just I'm not starting again.

MADISON	Your life.
KANE	Do you think less of me?
MADISON	For smoking?
KANE	For having had a boyfriend.
MADISON	You loved him?
KANE	I thought I did.
MADISON	So are you a straight man who fell in love with a gay guy a gay guy who decided to have a family or a bi guy with a rare sense of commitment?
KANE	I'm mostly straight.
MADISON	What about the whole born straight or born gay thing?
KANE	I don't think that applies to everyone.
MADISON	Where does Mom fit into this picture?

KANE lights another cigarette.

KANE	She we met after the breakup.
MADISON	But she always knew.
KANE	Of course. It wasn't a secret.
MADISON	When did you see him last?
KANE	The day I moved out.
MADISON	You don't wanna talk about this.
KANE	It doesn't matter anymore.
MADISON	Then why are you smoking again?

KANE   Because I'm scared my children hate me.

MADISON   I don't hate you.

KANE   Thanks.

MADISON   It was just you know.

KANE   I know.

>   *They embrace.*

MADISON   Now chuck those cigarettes before Ma gets a whiff of
            you.

>   *MADISON exits. A light rises on CAROLYN at the kitchen
>   table working on her laptop. ROYCE enters.*

CAROLYN   It's twelve forty-nine.

ROYCE   You should be in bed.

CAROLYN   I have to finish this payroll.

ROYCE   Is Dad asleep?

CAROLYN   Yeah. He's smoking again. Where were you?

ROYCE   Sigfreid's.

CAROLYN   Don't be angry at your father.

ROYCE   I'd prefer not to know anything about your sex lives.

CAROLYN   It was one short period of his life a long time ago.

ROYCE   We checked that guy out on the Net.

CAROLYN   Why would he be on the Net?

ROYCE   Everyone's on the Net. He's done porn.

CAROLYN   No. Really?

ROYCE   Totally. *Daddy Does Dallas* and *Wide Load in the Rear*. I downloaded a few stills if you want to.

CAROLYN   No thank you very much. I wish you'd stay away from that stuff.

ROYCE   Right. It's everywhere.

CAROLYN   I never would've thought—porn.

ROYCE   Jeez you act like there's something wrong with it.

CAROLYN   Isn't there?

ROYCE   Only if you're like really old. He's had quite a few restaurants too. Some really swish place in New York. Did you know him?

CAROLYN   Not really. Your father was in the process of breaking up with him when we met.

ROYCE   Were you the other woman?

CAROLYN   Don't be ridiculous. Go to bed. Now.

            Lights rise on DAVID *in the restaurant. He's testing fabrics for tablecloths and napkins against the colours of the room, muttering to himself.* MADISON *enters carrying a newspaper.*

MADISON   Hi.

DAVID   Hello—Madison?

MADISON   That's right.

DAVID   What can I do for you?

MADISON   I thought all the jobs were taken.

DAVID   They are.

MADISON   Then why are you still advertising for "waiter bus and
           bar staff"?

DAVID   The ad runs for a pre-set period.

MADISON   I think you're scared to hire me because you were my
           dad's boyfriend.

DAVID   They told you?

MADISON   Sure.

DAVID   Then I'm sure you can understand why I can't give you
           a job.

MADISON   Not really.

DAVID   It would be—uncomfortable.

MADISON   Because you're still in love with him?

DAVID   No.

MADISON   Then what's the problem?

DAVID   You're parents wouldn't approve.

MADISON   I'm a grown-up.

DAVID   It's a bad idea.

MADISON   They speak very highly of you.

DAVID   They do?

MADISON   Sounds like you were quite the influence.

DAVID   That's one way of putting it.

MADISON   How did you meet him?

DAVID   We worked at a restaurant. He was my busboy.

MADISON   Sounds romantic.

DAVID   It was fun.

MADISON   They were both delighted when I told them I'd met you.

DAVID   No they weren't.

MADISON   It was a long time ago. Everybody's over whatever happened by now right?

DAVID   You'd think so.

MADISON   They'd like to see you.

DAVID   Yeah right.

MADISON   I could probably get them to invite you for dinner.

DAVID   But you couldn't get me to come.

MADISON   You could meet my brother. See the whole family together. Then you'll be able to see there's no lingering whatevernesses and you can give me a job. Whadaya say?

DAVID   No. Now please go away and never bother me again.

        Pause.

MADISON   Now I see why he left you.

DAVID   Is that what he told you?

MADISON   Bye.

MADISON exits. Lights rise on the kitchen. ROYCE works with his laptop at the table. KANE and CAROLYN are preparing to go out.

ROYCE   Did you know we lost thirty percent of the polar ice cap last year?

CAROLYN   I'm not surprised.

KANE   It's so disturbing.

ROYCE   Polar bears are practically extinct.

KANE   Not to mention the suicide rate among the Inuit.

CAROLYN   Whose idea of after-dinner conversation is this?

ROYCE   I'm doing a report.

KANE   I watched a TV show.

MADISON enters.

MADISON   Sorry I'm late.

CAROLYN   You're supposed to call.

MADISON   My cell ran outa juice. Who died?

CAROLYN   For the opera.

MADISON   Ew.

ROYCE   Where were you?

MADISON   I went back to McMillan's restaurant.

KANE   Why?

MADISON   I need a job.

KANE   He already turned you down.

ROYCE   She was checking him out.

MADISON   I was so.

KANE   Madison.

MADISON   He won't give me the job because he thinks it would be a problem for you guys.

CAROLYN   It would be a problem for us guys.

MADISON   Why?

KANE   Because we don't want him back in our lives.

MADISON   Why would you think my working for him would bring him back into your lives?

KANE   Because he's David McMillan.

MADISON   I thought it might be nice if you guys asked him to dinner. Just to prove that—you know—everything's cool.

KANE   Forget it. You're not to go back there again. Ever. This subject is closed.

MADISON   Dad.

KANE   Closed.

            Very long pause.

ROYCE   He's got like a really fat dick.

KANE   Goddammit Royce.

            A light rises on DAVID in the restaurant. He is cleaning the bar and talking on his cellphone earpiece.

DAVID   I dreamed about him last night. It's strange. She
             doesn't really look like him but some of the things
             she says. The way she moves. I haven't dreamed about
             him in years. It was just short. We were in bed and he
             curled his back against my body the way he used to
             and I let my arm fall across his chest. I could feel him
             breathing. Then I woke up. Boring. Now tell me what's
             happening with you.

                    Lights rise on KANE *and* CAROLYN *walking to their car.*

CAROLYN   He practically winked at you.

KANE   Stop.

CAROLYN   He did. He said I hear David's back in town and then
             he all but winked at you. And the way Sylvia was
             smiling. Creepy.

KANE   If Maddy hadn't.

CAROLYN   But she did.

KANE   Why did he come back?

CAROLYN   I don't know but everyone in town's aware of it.

KANE   You're exaggerating.

CAROLYN   I know when people are talking about us. We have to
             do something.

KANE   What?

CAROLYN   Take Madison's suggestion to heart and invite him to
             dinner.

KANE   Seriously?

CAROLYN   Now that the cat's out of the bag we have no choice.

KANE   Sweetie it's a very bad idea.

CAROLYN   Would you rather wait to bump into him somewhere
            where we don't expect it? When we're both looking
            terrible?

KANE   Christ no.

CAROLYN   It's just dinner.

KANE   Right.

            Lights rise on MADISON *working on her laptop at the
            kitchen table.* ROYCE *enters and gets something to eat
            from the fridge.*

ROYCE   What're you doing?

MADISON   Family research.

ROYCE   What for?

MADISON   To see if there's anything else they're keeping from us.

ROYCE   And?

MADISON   And they are. You know those paternal grandparents
            we never met?

ROYCE   Died before we were born.

MADISON   Wrong. They didn't die until we were in school.

ROYCE   Why didn't Dad tell us about them?

MADISON   They seem to have completely disowned him.

ROYCE   Harsh.

MADISON   They were stinkin' rich.

ROYCE   No way.

MADISON   His dad was big in prescription-drug development.
             Left his entire fortune to a Christian family-values
             institution. You should see all the entries about our
             grandfather.

ROYCE   Seriously?

MADISON   I bet if Dad hadn't been a faggot we'd be living like
             millionaires right now.

ROYCE   Damn.

MADISON   He musta really loved that guy.

ROYCE   To give up your family like that.

MADISON   Doesn't seem like Dad.

ROYCE   You ever get the feeling they're really nothing like we
             think they are?

From the production at the Royal Exchange Theatre.
Amy Beth Hayes as Madison and Oliver Gomm as Royce.
Photograph by Jonathan Keenan.

MADISON   Yeah. Creepy.

ROYCE   Yeah.

            Lights rise on DAVID *reviewing a menu proof at a
            restaurant table.* KANE *and* CAROLYN *enter.*

KANE   Hi.

            Short pause.

DAVID   Kane.

CAROLYN   Hello David.

DAVID   Carolyn. Surprising to see you both. And so nicely
            turned out.

KANE   We were at the opera.

CAROLYN   *Così fan tutte.* Boring.

KANE   Hate opera.

CAROLYN   But a lot of our clients go.

DAVID   This is such a surprise.

KANE   We're here to apologize if Madison caused you any
            inconvenience.

DAVID   No problem. I probably would've hired her if she
            hadn't been your daughter.

KANE   We're grateful you didn't.

CAROLYN   This is a stunning room.

DAVID   I'll take that as a great compliment since I know you
            guys have one of the most successful interior-design
            firms in town.

CAROLYN   Don't you love googling?

DAVID   So much easier than small talk.

KANE   You designed this place yourself.

DAVID   You can tell?

KANE   Of course.

CAROLYN   Why's it called Mary's?

DAVID   My silent partner Mary Riley put up most of the
             money so she got naming rights.

CAROLYN   So you came back to—open a restaurant?

DAVID   I was looking for something to do.

CAROLYN   What happened to that fabulously successful place
             you had in New York?

DAVID   Everything goes out of style eventually. I've opened
             three other restaurants since then and now I'm right
             back where I started.

KANE   At least you're not a waiter.

DAVID   Really.

KANE   It's good to see you.

CAROLYN   Yes.

DAVID   Oddly—it's good to see you guys too.

KANE   Of course we wouldn't have come by if Maddy hadn't
             come in.

DAVID   We probably would've run into each other sooner or
             later.

KANE   Small world.

DAVID   And dying.

CAROLYN   Fate.

DAVID   You're well?

KANE   Yes.

DAVID   Are you happy?

KANE   What?

CAROLYN   Of course.

KANE   Yes.

CAROLYN   We're a happy family.

DAVID   Good.

CAROLYN   Are you single these days?

DAVID   Yes.

KANE   I'm surprised.

CAROLYN   You're such a catch.

DAVID   Still sampling the worms.

CAROLYN   We'd like to have you over for dinner.

DAVID   Really?

KANE   Yes.

CAROLYN   What better way could there be to say the past is behind us and we're all moving on to a new future? Come on. For old time's sake.

DAVID   Are you sure?

KANE   Of course.

CAROLYN   Say yes.

DAVID   Okay.

> *Lights rise on* MADISON *and* ROYCE *in the kitchen. She's packing up her laptop. He's getting more food from the fridge.*

ROYCE   Got any weed?

MADISON   Just a real long roach in my bag.

ROYCE   I could really use a toke.

MADISON   Why don't you have any?

> ROYCE *rubs his fingers at her indicating no money.*

I'll see what I can do.

> KANE *and* CAROLYN *enter.*

Hey.

ROYCE   What's happening?

KANE   Your mother just invited David McMillan to dinner.

MADISON   Really?

CAROLYN   Yes. Tomorrow.

MADISON   Why the change?

CAROLYN   Because you're absolutely right. What your father and David had has no bearing on our lives now. This dinner will prove that to everyone.

MADISON   Works for me.

ROYCE   Night.

KANE   Night kids.

MADISON and ROYCE exit.

CAROLYN   Does he still make your little heart go pitter pat?

KANE   He seemed.

CAROLYN   I know.

KANE   Not as.

CAROLYN   Intimidating.

KANE   Angry.

CAROLYN   But still.

KANE   Yes.

CAROLYN   He looked awfully good for fifty.

KANE   Tonight we should go for that quick bit of.

CAROLYN   Oh yeah.

A light rises on DAVID on his cellphone.

DAVID   He looked so—middle-aged. I warned him when we
               broke up time works differently in the straight world.
               And I hate to say it but she's held it together better
               than he has. Come on. That's a long time to hold a
               grudge and—honestly—now that I've seen them I
               think I got the better deal.

               *Lights rise on the kitchen. MADISON is there, checking
               the pots on the stove. ROYCE enters.*

MADISON   There's pâté in the fridge and some rice crackers over
            there.

ROYCE   Pâté?

MADISON   The pinky grey stuff that looks like ass barf from a sick
            dog.

ROYCE   I love that stuff. Where are they?

MADISON   Changing. Again.

ROYCE   Did you hear them last night?

MADISON   The fucking neighbours heard them.

ROYCE   Why are you dressed like a slut?

MADISON   Because I'm a slut.

ROYCE   I can see the tops of your aureoleos. *(or-ee-ole-eos)*

MADISON   Then look elsewhere pervert.

            KANE enters.

KANE   Well?

ROYCE   What?

MADISON   Better.

ROYCE   Did you get your hair dyed?

KANE   Just covered the grey and got some highlights.

            CAROLYN enters.

CAROLYN   Ta da.

ROYCE   Christ.

MADISON   Okay I'm just like whoa.

CAROLYN   I got a mini makeover. I couldn't help it.

ROYCE   This is weird.

MADISON   Really.

KANE   Maddy that shirt is not appropriate.

CAROLYN   A little cleavage is fine but.

KANE   I know you have a lot of other nice tops.

CAROLYN   That don't make you look like you're lactating. Change it.

MADISON   I have a right to express myself.

KANE   Listen to your mother.

MADISON   Style Nazis.

                    MADISON exits.

ROYCE   Is this alright?

KANE   You combed your hair.

ROYCE   Thinking about taking a shower too.

KANE   Don't get crazy.

CAROLYN   We can start moving the serving dishes to the table.

ROYCE   What is this?

CAROLYN   Thai Moroccan fusion.

ROYCE   Concept food.

CAROLYN   Be nice. I spent all day.

The doorbell rings.

KANE   I'll get it. I'll. Got it.

KANE exits.

ROYCE   What's with him?

CAROLYN   Nerves.

KANE   *(off)* Hey come in.

DAVID   *(off)* Thanks. How are you?

KANE   *(off)* Great. Thanks. Right through here.

DAVID   *(off)* Lovely place.

DAVID and KANE enter.

KANE   I'll give you a tour later.

DAVID   Hi.

CAROLYN   Welcome. You look wonderful.

DAVID   So do you.

DAVID and CAROLYN double cheek kiss stiffly.

CAROLYN   This is our son Royce.

DAVID   Hello Royce.

ROYCE   Hey.

DAVID   Fabulous kitchen. Very smart. The dining room is a thing of the past.

ROYCE   That's exactly what Dad said.

CAROLYN   Drink?

DAVID   What are you offering?

ROYCE   Jim Beam. They bought it special.

CAROLYN   Ice?

KANE   Lots just a splash of water.

DAVID   He mixed about two million of them when—back in the day.

CAROLYN   Kane?

KANE   Beer.

ROYCE   Me too.

CAROLYN   I don't.

KANE   A beer's fine.

DAVID   Where's Madison?

CAROLYN   She's changing.

ROYCE   Into someone less slutty.

DAVID   Why?

ROYCE   I saw you on the Net.

DAVID   Ah.

CAROLYN   Royce mentioned you'd done some—movies.

DAVID   Nothing worth discussing really.

ROYCE   Porn's completely legit. Don't be hung up.

DAVID   I'm not.

KANE   Royce.

DAVID   Carolyn let me give you a hand with those drinks.

CAROLYN   Here you go.

> DAVID *takes two beers and hands them to* KANE *and*
> ROYCE.

DAVID   Gentlemen.

KANE   Thank you.

CAROLYN   And this is for you.

DAVID   Aren't you having anything?

CAROLYN   I made myself a Singapore Sling.

ROYCE   There's a time vortex in our fridge.

DAVID   Royce tell me all about yourself.

ROYCE   What nothing no.

DAVID   What high-school stereotype do you fall into?

ROYCE   Angry outsider with a gift in cyber.

DAVID   Computers?

ROYCE   Are my bitch.

DAVID   I guess there's no point in asking if you've got a
             girlfriend.

KANE   Royce's shy with the girls.

ROYCE   They don't like me.

DAVID   There must be nerd girls that fancy you.

ROYCE   A couple. They're not very hot though.

DAVID   A satisfying sexual life is all about sliding standards. Just wear a condom. And if they're really unattractive take drugs.

CAROLYN   We're generally not quite so candid with our children.

DAVID   He conducts himself as an adult. I assumed you spoke to him like one.

CAROLYN   Not in that particular fashion.

ROYCE   My friend Sigfreid's dad has a twenty-two. We used it to go shoot some seagulls once. Have you ever hunted?

DAVID   Once or twice. Not really my thing.

ROYCE   It's kinda old school but I like the shooting.

            MADISON enters.

MADISON   Don't start without me.

CAROLYN   Madison.

KANE   That wasn't much of a change.

            MADISON moves to the counter to pour herself a drink.

MADISON   Best I could do.

KANE   You remember David.

MADISON   Of course.

DAVID   I think you all look wonderful.

CAROLYN   Really?

DAVID   A very handsome family.

CAROLYN   Everyone just help yourselves. So how is being back?

DAVID   Alright.

KANE   A lot of your old gang still around?

DAVID   No.

KANE   Why not?

DAVID   Between substance abuse and AIDS they're all pretty
             much drunk crazy or dead.

MADISON   That's sad.

DAVID   It's all just exposition now.

KANE   When's the restaurant opening?

DAVID   Two weeks. And we might actually be ready.

MADISON   Got all the staff you need?

CAROLYN   Now.

MADISON   Kidding.

DAVID   I told you.

MADISON   Why would they possibly object to you giving me a job?

CAROLYN   It's an—unhealthy lifestyle.

DAVID   Unhealthy lifestyle?

KANE   How is it?

DAVID   Delicious. Sort of Thai Moroccan.

CAROLYN   You're very good.

MADISON   Have you been single since you and my dad broke up?

DAVID   I've had—a few relationships.

CAROLYN   Anything that lasted?

DAVID   Six years is my record. One was a very well-known movie star but I can't tell you his name or we'll all be killed.

CAROLYN   Everyone's so surprised that you're back. Someone at the opera said they thought you'd retired somewhere warm a very rich man.

DAVID   I wish. My restaurants all did well. For a while. And I was rich. For a while.

ROYCE   What happened to all your money?

DAVID   I spent it on my cat.

KANE   Mr. Nippers?

DAVID   Yes.

CAROLYN   You know this cat?

KANE   I bought him for David when we moved in together.

MADISON   A little gay cat child. How touching.

DAVID   Sweet Mr. Nippers had a kidney infection thyroid condition and bowel dysfunction that cost me thousands of dollars the last ten years he was alive. Trying to keep a floundering restaurant afloat while medicating your cat eight times a day is no picnic.

CAROLYN   Much easier than children.

DAVID   And thankfully cats die at the same age most kids really start to resent their parents.

> MADISON *laughs.*

MADISON   Too true.

DAVID   And what are your long-term goals Madison?

MADISON   To never wear earrings that are too big for my face.

KANE   Maddy's good at so many things she always has trouble deciding.

CAROLYN   We think university might help her.

MADISON   Mother stop.

KANE   You've outdone yourself on dinner dear.

ROYCE   Not bad.

MADISON   She doesn't do this for just anyone.

ROYCE   Let alone the guy who useta do my dad.

KANE   Royce.

CAROLYN   Maddy have a bit more to eat.

MADISON   I'm not hungry.

ROYCE   She hardly ever eats.

MADISON   It's discipline not anorexia as the fat people are implying.

DAVID   I got that.

MADISON   It's quite inspiring the mature way you've all handled
            this reunion.

KANE   How else could we react?

DAVID   Times are different now.

MADISON   I bet a lot of people were freaked out about it at the
            time though.

KANE   You could say that.

MADISON   Is that why your parents disowned you?

            Pause.

KANE   Yes.

DAVID   Those people with the nice paintings disowned you?

KANE   Pretty much.

ROYCE   Why'd you tell us they were dead?

KANE   It was.

MADISON   Easier?

KANE   Yes.

CAROLYN   Unfortunately we never got the chance to repair that
            rift.

KANE   There was no repairing that rift.

CAROLYN   They would've forgiven you.

KANE   Never.

CAROLYN   In time. If they'd met the children.

KANE   You didn't know them.

MADISON   They sound like horrid people.

KANE   They were.

DAVID   Kane I'm sorry.

CAROLYN   I could've made them understand.

ROYCE   Understand what?

CAROLYN   That Kane's whole thing with David wasn't real.

              Pause.

DAVID   Real?

CAROLYN   Did I say that?

DAVID   Yes.

CAROLYN   I didn't mean real—

DAVID   Good.

CAROLYN   It just wasn't—you know—like with a man and woman.
              It was different. That's what I meant. Different. Isn't
              that right?

KANE   What?

CAROLYN   It was different.

KANE   Everything's different.

CAROLYN   Kane wasn't really gay. Not that that invalidates your
              relationship in any way. But he has a family now so I
              guess that proves something right?

KANE   Carolyn.

CAROLYN   This isn't coming out the way it's supposed to.

MADISON   Then why don't you stop?

Long pause.

KANE   Who wants seconds?

DAVID   I should go.

CAROLYN   I didn't mean to offend you.

DAVID   I'm not offended. I still have work to do tonight.

KANE   Okay.

DAVID   Thank you so much for dinner.

CAROLYN   It's what we'd do for any old friend.

Short pause.

DAVID   You know Madison is right. If we're such good old friends there's absolutely no reason I shouldn't hire her at the restaurant.

MADISON   You serious?

DAVID   Show up for training at two tomorrow.

MADISON   Thank you.

DAVID   You're welcome. Thanks again for the terrific dinner.

DAVID exits.

ROYCE   What just happened?

MADISON   I got the job.

CAROLYN   I will not allow it.

KANE   It's a bad idea.

              MADISON laughs and clears the table.

MADISON   I got the job. I got the job.

              A light rises on DAVID at the restaurant on his cell.

DAVID   How old are you? Perfect. I'm—forty. You like older
              guys. Good. What's your name? I'm Ted. Are you alone
              Jacob? Good. What are you wearing? Great. So tell me
              what you like Jacob. No. We don't have to have phone
              sex. I guess I'm cool to just talk if that's what you want.
              Sure.

              *Lights rise on CAROLYN, dressed for bed. She's brushing
              her hair in the mirror. KANE is changing into his pyjamas
              as they speak.*

CAROLYN   Talk her out of it.

KANE   You know how that works with her.

From the production at Factory Theatre.
Julie Stewart as Carolyn, Susanna Fournier as Madison and Andrew Craig as Royce.
Photograph by Ed Gass-Donnelly.

CAROLYN   Nothing good will come of it.

KANE   Well if you hadn't been so.

CAROLYN   What?

KANE   Outspoken.

CAROLYN   I didn't mean for that to come out like that. I just—he
            was the one with all the excitement and glamour.

KANE   It wasn't that exciting or glamorous. You don't know
            what it's like playing second fiddle to someone all the
            time.

CAROLYN   Is that why you married me?

KANE   Honey please.

CAROLYN   There's a look in your eye. A place you go sometimes
            when you think no one's looking. I know you're
            thinking about him. I've always known.

KANE   You've got to let this go.

CAROLYN   It's not something I ever understood. It doesn't seem
            like you. To do that. With a man. It just doesn't seem
            real.

KANE   We made a mistake. Inviting him here. Let's admit
            that and get on with it. We don't have to see him again.
            Madison might even hate the job.

            KANE kisses CAROLYN.

CAROLYN   You're absolutely right. I'm sorry.

            KANE moves closer to her.

KANE   I have an idea for how you can make it up to me.

Lights rise on DAVID *at the restaurant going through the reservation book.* MADISON *enters in waiter gear.*

MADISON   You wanted to see me?

DAVID   I hear your training's going quite well.

MADISON   Who knew you had to know so much to be a waiter?

DAVID   This job hasn't created a rift at home has it?

MADISON   Everyone seems to be getting over it.

DAVID   Good. We're opening tomorrow night and I just—I want you to know that you'll be judged like any other waiter.

MADISON   You mean you're not going to cut me any slack just because you gave me the job to piss my mother off?

DAVID   I wouldn't have put it quite that way but sure.

MADISON   I'm going to be very good.

DAVID   You'd better be.

MADISON   Just watch.

MADISON exits. Light rise on the kitchen. KANE, CAROLYN *and* ROYCE *setting food on the dinner table.*

CAROLYN   Dinner.

They sit and eat in silence for a longish moment.

ROYCE   Sigfreid rimmed me last night.

KANE   Son please don't say rimmed at the dinner table.

CAROLYN   Thank you Kane.

ROYCE   I thought personal sexual revelations over dinner are what we're all about.

KANE   Royce.

CAROLYN   I liked it so much better when you were obsessed with *Warmonger*.

ROYCE   That was before my childhood had been shattered. At least now I understand why I'm so weird.

CAROLYN   Somewhere there are a whole bunch of girls just waiting for a boy like you.

ROYCE   Never invite me to that party.

CAROLYN   You've got to stop putting yourself down.

ROYCE   I'm just beating everyone else to it.

KANE   It won't always be like this.

ROYCE   Right. I'm still the ugly geek they all laugh at.

CAROLYN   Who laughs at you?

ROYCE   Forget it.

KANE   Is it really that bad?

ROYCE   No.

KANE   If there's a serious problem you need to tell us.

ROYCE   No serious problems. Everything's fine.

Pause.

CAROLYN   Have some more carrots. I made way too many carrots.

ROYCE   No.

ROYCE *exits. Pause.*

CAROLYN   Carrots?

KANE   No.

              They eat in silence. A light rises on DAVID *at the restaurant, eating.* MADISON *enters.*

MADISON   Eating alone's a drag.

DAVID   I'm used to it.

MADISON   Good night.

DAVID   Things look promising but we won't really know how we're doing for a few months. Where have all the waiters gone?

MADISON   Comfort for last call.

DAVID   Not joining them?

MADISON   The bar's fun once in a while but I don't like to make it a habit.

DAVID   You're too young to be so responsible.

MADISON   What do you do when you leave here?

DAVID   Meet with Mary think about what needs to be done tomorrow watch the news.

MADISON   You don't go to the bars?

DAVID   I used to. Every night for twenty-five years. All over the world. It was wonderful. But these last few years. Over forty and you're invisible.

MADISON   Don't you even like drive around and pick up men on the street or cruise the parks or bathrooms or whatever?

DAVID   That's not really my scene.

MADISON   So you just watch the news?

DAVID   You sound disappointed.

MADISON   We could go meet the other waiters for a drink.

DAVID   I'm bushed.

MADISON   You sure?

DAVID   Positive. Thanks for asking.

MADISON   Good night.

> *MADISON clears the table quickly and exits. Lights rise on* ROYCE *in his bedroom, on his computer. There's a knock.*

ROYCE   What?

> *KANE enters.*

KANE   Turn the computer off.

ROYCE   Dad I'm.

KANE   Off.

> ROYCE *turns the computer off.*

You have every right to be confused.

ROYCE   I'm not confused. You're the popular guy who gets to have sex with everyone.

KANE   It wasn't all about sex.

ROYCE   Oh right. You loved him.

KANE   Does that bother you?

ROYCE   Why would I care?

KANE   Because I'm not the man you thought I was.

ROYCE   I got over that when I was thirteen.

KANE   I don't understand why you're so cynical. We've tried
          to understand. Helped where we could.

ROYCE   I know.

KANE   But lately it's like you have to ridicule everything I say.
          Fudgepacker this and buttboy that and he rimmed me.
          It's getting old.

ROYCE   I'm just kidding around.

KANE   It's not funny.

ROYCE   I don't get it okay. I just don't.

KANE   It's not as simple as they make it sound Royce. Not
          for everyone. Some people respond to members of the
          same sex some respond to members of the opposite
          sex and.

ROYCE   Some are bi. I know the score. Jeez Dad.

KANE   Even saying bi is a simplification. It's not about labels
          it's about individuals. Does that make any sense?

ROYCE   No.

KANE   Sometimes people meet and whatever they share goes
          beyond sexuality.

ROYCE   Sounds romantic.

KANE   I'm not going to go around acting like I'm ashamed if
             that's what you want. Love sex all of that. It's not so
             easy. You'll see someday.

ROYCE   Doubtful. Does Mom have any deep dark secrets we
             don't know about?

KANE   No.

                     MADISON enters.

MADISON   Party?

KANE   I was just heading to bed.

MADISON   Everything okay?

KANE   Fine. Night.

                     KANE exits.

MADISON   What's with him?

ROYCE   He's still worried we hate him.

MADISON   Do you?

ROYCE   He's Dad.

MADISON   Doesn't mean it's easy to get used to.

ROYCE   Whatever how was work?

                     MADISON flashes ROYCE a wad of bills.

MADISON   I'd say pretty fucking good.

ROYCE   Nice. Man do I need a job. Or a life. Or a shot to the
             head or something.

Pause.

MADISON   What's the baby brother bummed about?

ROYCE   Fuck off.

MADISON   Royce.

ROYCE   I keep having dreams about finding my family hanging
            in the basement with their throats slit and their
            intestines pulled through wounds in their bellies. And
            sometimes when I'm watching TV by myself I start
            crying and I don't know why and the show's not even
            sad or whatever.

            Pause.

MADISON   Are you trying to come out to me?

ROYCE   No.

MADISON   It's alright if you are.

ROYCE   I'm not. Now get out.

            Lights rise on DAVID restocking the bar, on the cellphone.

DAVID   Marcelle I need another two cases of the Zinfandel
            you sold me last week. Yeah I sold out. If you ate here
            once in a while you'd know why. Next time you're in
            talk to me and we'll book something for you—on the
            house. Great. Two cases.

            ROYCE enters.

            Hey.

ROYCE   Madison done yet?

DAVID   She might be a while.

ROYCE   Thought I'd give her a ride home.

DAVID   On a Friday night?

ROYCE   Yeah.

DAVID   That's tragic.

ROYCE   Yeah what's up with you?

DAVID   This is my life.

             Pause.

             Do you want a coffee or something?

ROYCE   I'm fine.

DAVID   I have to finish restocking the bar.

ROYCE   Can I give you a hand?

DAVID   Thanks. It's okay.

             Pause as ROYCE *watches* DAVID *work.*

ROYCE   Why'd you do that shit on the Net?

DAVID   The porn?

ROYCE   Yeah.

DAVID   I was—proving something.

ROYCE   What?

DAVID   That AIDS didn't have the power to ruin my sex life.

ROYCE   Who were you proving it to?

DAVID   Myself. Everyone. I don't know. It was a pretty messed-
             up time. Honestly I needed the money.

ROYCE   They pay you a lot?

DAVID   I don't think your mother would approve of this
             conversation.

ROYCE   That's why I'm having it with you.

DAVID   You're the computer dude. You've seen worse.

ROYCE   Oh yeah. Chicks with dicks guys with pies pop on top
             K-9 brown-eye. Everything.

DAVID   I guess finding out about me is nothing compared to—
             whatever it was you just said.

ROYCE   I dunno. Like some stuff makes sense now.

DAVID   Such as?

ROYCE   He was never like other dads.

DAVID   No?

ROYCE   Too creative and smart. And he's into antiques and
             shit. Fabrics. He loves fabrics. But he's not femmy.
             Most guys like that are femmy.

DAVID   Is he a good father?

ROYCE   In a boring good-father way can I have a job?

                     Pause.

DAVID   It would be—awkward with Madison here.

ROYCE   Why?

DAVID   I can't have outside—family—issues creeping into work.

ROYCE   Sure.

DAVID   Besides.

ROYCE   What?

DAVID   You're too bright. Bright busboys are always a pain in the ass because they know how much their job sucks. Why don't I go see what's keeping your sister?

ROYCE   Okay great thanks.

> *DAVID exits. A light rises on* MADISON *in the kitchen making pancakes.* CAROLYN *is at the table drinking coffee and reading the paper.*

MADISON   Two or four?

CAROLYN   Two. Your father will want four and Royce will have six but only eat five. I can't believe you're doing this after getting in at three thirty-seven.

MADISON   I thought it would be nice.

CAROLYN   What do you do after closing?

MADISON   Hang out for drinks and talk.

CAROLYN   With who?

MADISON   The other waiters staff whoever.

CAROLYN   David?

MADISON   Once in a while.

CAROLYN   Dad's assistant quit.

KANE enters.

KANE   She's going on some reality show and they need to rehearse for two months.

MADISON   Reality's not what it used to be.

KANE   Interested in the position?

MADISON   Not an iota.

MADISON serves them pancakes.

KANE   What time did Royce get in?

CAROLYN   Twelve thirteen.

MADISON   Do you ever sleep?

CAROLYN   An hour here and there.

MADISON   Bacon?

KANE   I can't.

MADISON   It's turkey bacon.

KANE   I really can't.

CAROLYN   I will.

ROYCE enters.

ROYCE   Could everyone please talk louder.

CAROLYN   Good morning.

MADISON   I made pancakes.

ROYCE   Yippee.

MADISON   With a raspberry compote.

ROYCE   Compote?

KANE   With a splash of Grand Marnier?

MADISON   Yeah.

CAROLYN   David taught you how to make that.

MADISON   How did you know?

CAROLYN   Your father made it for me once. On our honeymoon.
           I later found out it was David's favourite.

KANE   Nobody doesn't like raspberry compote.

MADISON   He did suggest it.

CAROLYN   Of course.

                    They all eat.

ROYCE   Wow.

KANE   That's very good.

CAROLYN   I prefer good old-fashioned maple syrup myself.

ROYCE   Is this fucking turkey bacon?

CAROLYN   After breakfast we're going to see Grandpa Carver.

KANE   Are we?

MADISON   Why?

ROYCE   He keeps calling me Ronnie.

CAROLYN   That was.

ROYCE   His brother. Yeah.

MADISON   I hate the smell of that place.

ROYCE   He always cries when he sees us.

CAROLYN   Because he loves us so much.

MADISON   Because he knows we put him in there.

CAROLYN   He likes to see us as a family.

MADISON   He doesn't know who we are.

KANE   Your mother's right. We should do more together. The
               drive will be nice.

ROYCE   Our visits mean nothing to him.

CAROLYN   But they mean a lot to me.

                    MADISON's cellphone rings.

MADISON   Hi David. Really. Well. Okay. No problem. Great.

CAROLYN   What?

MADISON   The coke addict called in sick again.

KANE   You have to work.

CAROLYN   What will we tell Grandpa?

MADISON   Anything you want. He won't remember. I've gotta get
               some zees.

CAROLYN   Who's cleaning up?

MADISON   Anyone who didn't cook. And I'm taking your car.

                    MADISON exits.

KANE   I'll get the dishes.

CAROLYN   Aren't you going to come up with some excuse too?

ROYCE   You kidding? Grandpa Carver's the only person who
            can make me feel alright about my social life.

KANE   You can drive.

ROYCE   Great.

            Lights rise on DAVID *going through the reservation
            book.* MADISON *is there.*

DAVID   You saved the day.

MADISON   You saved me from a trip to see Grandpa Carver.

DAVID   We won't be seeing Max again.

MADISON   He was stealing from the bar.

DAVID   Drug addicts always are.

MADISON   I was going to tell you.

DAVID   That's not your responsibility.

MADISON   So.

            Pause.

DAVID   Go ahead.

MADISON   When I was driving here. It just kinda hit me. I mean
            I'd never really considered it before and I was just
            kinda—I don't know.

DAVID   What are you talking about?

MADISON   You fucked my father.

Pause.

DAVID   Why would you think about that?

MADISON   Uh—you were lovers.

DAVID   Jesus Madison.

MADISON   Well?

DAVID   Let's just say people with really nice bums usually get them for a reason.

                 MADISON laughs.

                 That's not quite the reaction I expected.

MADISON   Please. Ass is the new vagina.

DAVID   Charming.

MADISON   How do you think all those uptight girls manage to stay "virgins" until they get married. And I've never dated a guy who didn't eventually try to get me to insert something—anything really—into his butt.

DAVID   Straight people are always stealing our best ideas.

MADISON   Was he always the bottom?

DAVID   Quit asking so many questions about your father and get to work.

MADISON   Yes sir.

                 MADISON salutes and exits. Lights rise on ROYCE, CAROLYN and KANE walking to the car.

CAROLYN   I wish he'd die.

KANE   Honey.

CAROLYN   If he knew what he was doing he'd want to.

ROYCE   That was so majorly disgusting.

KANE   It's a terrible disease.

CAROLYN   He lectured on Chaucer and gave tony cocktail parties for visiting writers.

ROYCE   Seriously?

CAROLYN   I know he'd rather be dead.

ROYCE   We should kill him.

KANE   Stop.

ROYCE   It's what he'd want.

KANE   We don't know what he wants.

ROYCE   So you're saying if you ever become a drooling idiot who pulls his dick out and cranks it whenever your family comes to visit you don't want us to kill you?

           Pause.

KANE   Shut up.

ROYCE   But really.

CAROLYN   I wish he'd die.

KANE   I'd want you to kill me.

           Lights rise on the restaurant. DAVID is closing up the bar. MADISON enters with two plates of food.

MADISON   Sorry about the salmon controversy.

DAVID   Everyone makes mistakes.

MADISON   Not me.

DAVID   Even you.

MADISON   And you?

DAVID   I've made many mistakes.

MADISON   Like Dad?

DAVID   You're supposed to stop asking about him.

MADISON   Sorry but parents are so strange.

DAVID   They're just people.

MADISON   What about yours?

DAVID   I'm the illegitimate offspring of Wonder Woman and
            the Empire State Building.

MADISON   But really.

DAVID   Haven't seen them in years.

MADISON   Why not?

DAVID   Not really my kind of people.

MADISON   It's got to be hard to give up a family. Even a bad one.

DAVID   It's how fags escape from the trailer parks and small
            towns of their white-trash boyhoods.

MADISON   They're your family. You're supposed to love each
            other forever.

DAVID   There are very few relationships that are meant to
            last forever. And if they do it's never without major
            renovation.

MADISON   Everyone I know's terrified of their relationship failing.

DAVID   Just because a relationship's over doesn't mean it's failed.

MADISON   I hope to have a relationship some day.

DAVID   You will.

MADISON   With someone bright and well-hung?

DAVID   It's not impossible but relatively rare.

CAROLYN   You want to come to Comfort?

DAVID   It's not good form for management to party with the staff.

MADISON   Fuck good form. It'll let everyone know you're not as uptight as you seem.

DAVID   Uptight?

MADISON   A coupla drinks.

DAVID   Who's going?

MADISON   Marvin Willett Debra everyone.

ROYCE *enters.*

DAVID   Hi Royce.

MADISON   I told you to call before you came by.

ROYCE   I was in the hood.

MADISON   I'm going out.

ROYCE   Oh okay sorry. You need a ride?

DAVID   I'm fine thanks.

                        Short pause.

ROYCE   Alright.

                        ROYCE exits.

DAVID   You could've invited him.

MADISON   No way. You coming?

DAVID   Yeah sure.

                        *Lights rise on CAROLYN in bed, reading. KANE enters
                        from the bathroom wearing his pyjama bottoms.*

KANE   This belly's getting out of control.

CAROLYN   You've still got a nice ass.

KANE   You're the one who kept her body.

CAROLYN   Except for my saggy tits.

KANE   You'll always be that same hot girl Attila introduced
                me to at the Drink Exchange.

CAROLYN   That girl and her perky tits are gone.

                        *KANE stops in front of the mirror to pluck some shoulder
                        hairs.*

KANE   Not in my eyes.

CAROLYN   Any sign of the kids?

KANE   No.

CAROLYN   Royce has the car?

KANE   Gets him outa the fucking house for a change.

CAROLYN   What do you think he does?

KANE   Drives around listening to music and thinking about
                himself.

CAROLYN   And Madison?

KANE   She's making a million new friends and trying a million
                new things. Let's just leave it at that. Check my back
                for hairs.

From the production at the Royal Exchange Theatre.
Teresa Banham as Carolyn and John Kirk as Kane.
Photograph by Jonathan Keenan.

CAROLYN inspects KANE's back.

CAROLYN   It's all just so.

KANE   What are we going to do?

CAROLYN   Do?

KANE   When they're gone.

CAROLYN   I don't know.

KANE   It'll be strange.

CAROLYN   Like starting over again.

CAROLYN pulls a hair out.

KANE   Ow. Yeah.

CAROLYN   It's really.

KANE   I know.

CAROLYN   I mean really.

KANE   I know.

Lights rise on DAVID and MADISON on the street. They're searching for a cab, both a bit drunk.

DAVID   I'll hail you a cab.

MADISON   I have them on speed-dial.

MADISON speed-dials her cellphone.

MADISON   I need a cab at Comfort. Great.

DAVID   How long?

MADISON   Pretty quick. We're downtown.

DAVID   I'll wait with you.

MADISON   It's okay.

DAVID   At this time of night? I'll wait.

MADISON   You should head off to some corn-holing festival.

DAVID   No thanks.

MADISON   You're alone too much.

DAVID   I'm fine.

MADISON   I worry about you.

DAVID   Don't.

MADISON   When was the last time you saw Dad?

DAVID   Montreal.

MADISON   Really?

DAVID   A year or so after we'd broken up. I was opening a swank room while learning French and he was buying antiques or something. We ran into each other on St. Catherine.

MADISON   Big coincidence?

DAVID   My life's like that.

MADISON   Did you talk?

DAVID   Briefly. Here comes your cab.

MADISON   I had fun.

DAVID   Me too.

             MADISON gives DAVID a sudden kiss. It lingers for a
             moment before DAVID steps out of it.

             Your cab.

MADISON   Yeah. Over here.

DAVID   Good night.

MADISON   Night.

             Lights rise on CAROLYN in the kitchen making cocoa.
             MADISON enters.

CAROLYN   Two forty-three.

MADISON   Mom I think Royce is like really depressed or something.

CAROLYN   What makes you say that?

MADISON   Aren't you aware of how much time he spends alone?
             He has no friends.

CAROLYN   He has friends on the Net.

MADISON   Net friends aren't real.

CAROLYN   What about Sigfreid?

MADISON   He hardly sees him anymore.

CAROLYN   What do you want me to do?

MADISON   Someone needs to talk to him.

CAROLYN   I've tried to get him to open up. So has your father.

MADISON   He keeps coming by work at inappropriate times. I
             think he's trying to reach out or something.

CAROLYN   Are you that concerned?

MADISON   He's having nightmares and crying jags. Don't you hear him at night?

CAROLYN   I thought he was—masturbating.

MADISON   Mother.

CAROLYN   I'll talk to your father.

MADISON   As soon as possible.

CAROLYN   Okay.

MADISON   Go to bed.

CAROLYN   I'll never get to sleep now.

> *Lights rise on* DAVID *walking to his apartment building.* ROYCE *is sitting on the steps.*

DAVID   Royce?

ROYCE   Hey.

DAVID   This is a surprise.

ROYCE   I didn't have anywhere else to go.

> *Pause.*

DAVID   Have you followed me here before?

ROYCE   You went out with my sister.

DAVID   We met some people for drinks.

ROYCE   You like her?

DAVID   Yes.

ROYCE   Everyone likes her.

DAVID   She's very personable.

ROYCE   Why am I a loser?

DAVID   The losers in school are the ones who prove themselves in adulthood.

ROYCE   Were you a loser in high school?

DAVID   No.

ROYCE   They laugh at me.

DAVID   Who?

ROYCE   All of them. They always have. They call me names. Push me into my locker. Knock my books out of my hands. Punch me in the face after they have a fight with their girlfriends. Shove my head in the toilet if they catch me in the can.

DAVID   You need to stand up to them.

ROYCE   Like I could ever do that and live.

DAVID   Transfer schools.

ROYCE   I've done that. I still end up being the geek everyone picks on. It started in the first grade and never really stopped.

DAVID   What do you plan to do when you're finished school?

ROYCE   Be one of those guys who lives in their parents' basement until they're forty.

DAVID   That's your plan?

ROYCE   It's more like a destiny.

DAVID   What do you really enjoy?

ROYCE   I don't—computer games I guess.

DAVID   Okay. Good. So concentrate on computer games. Design them. Change them.

ROYCE   I suck at creative shit.

             Pause.

DAVID   I don't know what else to say.

ROYCE   There's something wrong with me.

DAVID   Wrong how?

ROYCE   I'm like beyond average. Super average or something.

DAVID   Adulthood is different. You can move somewhere else and completely reinvent yourself. A number of times if you have to. Find someone else to emulate. Adopt traits you find attractive in others. It can be done. Trust me.

ROYCE   People shouldn't tell ordinary kids they're special. It fucks them up when they get older and realize they're not special.

             Pause.

DAVID   Royce it's very late.

ROYCE   Do you want me to come up?

DAVID   Come up?

ROYCE   To your apartment.

DAVID   For what?

ROYCE   Talking whatever.

DAVID   You should go home.

           Pause.

ROYCE   If I was a hot guy you would've hired me.

DAVID   And if I was a beautiful woman I'd be a movie star.
           What's your point?

ROYCE   Nothing night thanks.

DAVID   Take it easy.

           *ROYCE exits. DAVID watches him leave. A light rises
           on KANE waiting in the kitchen, drinking a beer and
           smoking a cigarette in front of the open window. ROYCE
           enters. KANE tosses the cigarette out the window.*

ROYCE   Aren't you afraid of giving all of us cancer?

KANE   Your mother is upstairs trying to convince herself you
           haven't been killed in an accident.

ROYCE   Lost track.

KANE   Where did you go?

ROYCE   Nowhere.

KANE   You know you're not supposed to have the car out this
           late.

ROYCE   I buy gas.

KANE   I think you should—talk to a professional.

ROYCE   Professional what?

KANE   Counsellor or therapist.

ROYCE   You think I'm crazy.

KANE	I think you might need some.
ROYCE	I don't.
KANE	We're your family.
ROYCE	I'm nothing like you people.
KANE	You're part of us.
ROYCE	You're pissed.
KANE	I've had three beers.
ROYCE	I'm fine.
KANE	What's the harm in talking to someone?
ROYCE	I don't want to.
KANE	I know you've been having a rough time.
ROYCE	You don't know anything.
KANE	There are issues.
ROYCE	There are no fucking issues.
KANE	Things we should.
ROYCE	I'm not discussing anything with anyone.
KANE	What do you want me to do?
ROYCE	Make me not ugly. Teach me to understand how people work.
KANE	You're not ugly.
ROYCE	Quit lying to me.

CAROLYN enters.

CAROLYN   Everything okay?

ROYCE   Dad's acting creepy.

KANE   Stop it.

CAROLYN   You can't use the car anymore.

ROYCE   Like I care.

> *ROYCE exits.*

CAROLYN   I can tell that went well.

KANE   He's got a terrible attitude.

CAROLYN   You know confrontation doesn't work with him.

KANE   I did my best.

> *KANE moves to exit.*

CAROLYN   Where are you going?

KANE   Outside for a cigarette.

CAROLYN   Fine.

> *Lights rise on* MADISON *setting tables at the restaurant.* DAVID *is setting plates of food and a carafe of wine on another table.*

DAVID   Shrimp sautéed in garlic and olive oil over penne. And wine.

MADISON   Sounds great.

DAVID   It was the least I could do after you picked up those extra tables.

MADISON joins DAVID.

MADISON   Who knew Alena would have a meltdown?

DAVID   She's pregnant poor thing.

MADISON   Bummer. Delicious. Wow.

DAVID   Don't let it go to your head but I think you do an amazing job on the floor Maddy.

MADISON   Blame it on the fascist who runs the dump.

DAVID   Quality counts.

MADISON   You ever had sex with a woman?

DAVID   You have no internal censor at all do you?

MADISON   No so?

DAVID   A few. Not in a very long time.

MADISON   I've had sex with a couple women.

DAVID   Good for you.

MADISON   I guess that's why I didn't freak out when I found out about Dad and you. I know what it's like to want to try different things.

DAVID   Your father's daughter.

MADISON   Gay is so over. The word doesn't really mean anything anymore. Like Negro or Jewess. It's all just sex. I could probably have a relationship with a girl. If she had a cock. I really like cock.

DAVID   Who doesn't?

MADISON   When I was fifteen I got this crush on this client of my dad's. He was this divorced guy in his mid-thirties.

DAVID   An older man.

MADISON   We used to meet at this hotel once a week and fuck like pigs. He told the staff I was his niece. I told my folks I was tutoring retards for extra karma. He moved to San Diego and married some fucking telephone exec bitch his own age my graduating year. I was like functionally depressed for eight months. Really.

DAVID   Why don't you go out with boys your own age?

MADISON   They're really bad sex.

DAVID   You have to teach them what to do.

MADISON   Get a hooker. I think I'm a fag. In a woman's body. I understand you guys too well. I get it. Well not some of those old singers but the sex and everything else. I get it.

DAVID   Why are you telling me all this?

MADISON   Because I really want to fuck you.

                 Pause.

DAVID   I'm—management.

MADISON   David.

DAVID   I'm gay.

MADISON   Doesn't mean anything.

                 MADISON *begins to move toward* DAVID.

DAVID   I don't even know if.

MADISON   You've done porn.

DAVID   Stay back.

            MADISON puts her arms around DAVID's neck.

MADISON   I have condoms.

DAVID   You're only doing this because of my connection to your father.

MADISON   I prefer men who are nothing like my father.

            Pause.

DAVID   This isn't real.

MADISON   What is?

            They kiss suddenly and passionately. They begin to undo one another's clothes. Fade to black.

ACT TWO

Lights rise on DAVID *and* MADISON *sprawled across a table, sweaty and dishevelled, breathing heavily, partially dressed.* DAVID *gets off of her. They straighten their clothing, close zippers, locate panties, dispose of the condom, etc. Neither speaks. Finally.*

DAVID   So.

MADISON   Yeah.

Pause.

DAVID   How was I?

MADISON   Not bad. For a fag.

DAVID   You seem.

MADISON   It's alright.

DAVID   Really?

MADISON   Really.

                    Pause.

DAVID   I should.

MADISON   Yes.

DAVID   Good.

MADISON   Okay.

DAVID   Everything's?

MADISON   Fine fine.

                    KANE enters.

KANE   Madison.

MADISON   Daddy?

DAVID   Kane.

KANE   Do you have any idea what time it is?

MADISON   No.

DAVID   We got.

MADISON   Talking.

KANE   Your mother's very.

MADISON   I can't believe you'd come here like this.

KANE   There was no answer on your cell.

MADISON   I turn it off at work.

KANE   We should.

MADISON   I've got Mom's car.

KANE   Go ahead.

                    MADISON exits.

              You okay?

DAVID   Yeah fine why?

KANE   I dunno. You look kinda—funny.

DAVID   I'm just tired.

KANE   That night at dinner. I hope you didn't take what
              Carolyn said the wrong way. She didn't mean to hurt
              your feelings or anything like that.

DAVID   I know.

KANE   Everyone puts their foot in their mouth once in a
              while right?

DAVID   Right. Kane—how is your relationship with your kids?

KANE   Good. Why?

DAVID   They just seem to.

KANE   What?

DAVID   They like to talk.

KANE   To you?

DAVID   Yeah.

KANE   I want to talk to them. I try. But they just don't seem
              interested. Royce gets further away all the time.

DAVID   It's a challenge.

KANE   Has he told you something he hasn't told me that might make everything alright?

DAVID   Nope.

KANE   Damn.

                 Pause.

                 David please fire Madison. Please.

DAVID   I can't.

KANE   Something—this is really messing up my family. Ever since she started working here.

DAVID   I can't fire someone because their parents are uncomfortable. There are laws against that kind of thing now.

KANE   Can't you find some excuse?

DAVID   Unfortunately she's an excellent waiter.

KANE   Shit.

DAVID   We're stuck for the time being.

KANE   She shouldn't be working here.

DAVID   I've come to agree.

KANE   And there's nothing you can do?

DAVID   I wish there were.

KANE   You had no business coming back here.

DAVID   I didn't have a lot of other options.

KANE   I know how interesting things get when you show up.
              I don't want things to get interesting.

DAVID   I didn't want to see you any more than you wanted to
              see me.

KANE   Okay. Good. Great.

DAVID   And I promise if I can find a way to let Madison go I'll
              do it.

KANE   I'd appreciate it.

DAVID   And our paths will never intersect again.

KANE   Great.

              *KANE exits. DAVID sits at the table and pours himself a
              large glass of wine. Lights rise on CAROLYN cleaning the
              sink in the kitchen. MADISON enters.*

CAROLYN   There are only two reasons anyone stays out until this
              time of the morning and they are sex and drugs.

MADISON   I have a right to my own life.

CAROLYN   You don't have the right to keep us up all night.

MADISON   Okay. True. It's time I.

CAROLYN   Move out?

MADISON   I'm making enough money to get my own place.

CAROLYN   If you get your own place you'll never go back to school.

MADISON   People do it all the time.

CAROLYN   It's very hard.

MADISON   Mom you've been hinting for me to move out of here for a year. Why are you changing that now?

CAROLYN   I'm not.

MADISON   Are you in menopause or something?

CAROLYN   THERE'S NOTHING WRONG WITH ME!

                        Long pause.

MADISON   Sit down.

CAROLYN   I'm.

MADISON   Sit.

                        CAROLYN sits.

CAROLYN   Sorry I didn't sorry.

MADISON   You were totally unhinged for a second there.

CAROLYN   I'm just overtired. Really.

MADISON   What's going on?

CAROLYN   Don't listen to me. Move out. Get your own place. Have a life. It's important.

MADISON   I'll make some tea.

CAROLYN   Don't bother sweetie. I'm okay.

MADISON   What's with you?

CAROLYN   I don't know. I can't sleep—can't shake this feeling there's something I'm supposed to be doing— something that I keep missing.

MADISON   What is it?

CAROLYN   I was raised to get married as soon as I finished school.
             It's what my mother did. It's what her mother did. I
             never even questioned it.

MADISON   Are you now?

CAROLYN   I'm not sure what I'm supposed to do next.

MADISON   Everything you put off when you got married.

CAROLYN   But I didn't put anything off. Marriage was all I wanted.
             I assumed everything would be like my mother and
             father.

MADISON   Was their marriage that great?

CAROLYN   Probably not but the fact that she died so young added
             a certain mythical quality to it. I mean no one got to
             find out how she would've reacted when her kids grew
             up and she had nothing to focus on.

MADISON   Have you talked to Dad about this?

CAROLYN   He sees us going to Florida a lot and playing golf.

MADISON   Golf?

CAROLYN   Apparently after a certain age everyone's supposed to
             like it. It's like exercise without any effort.

MADISON   That's horrifying.

CAROLYN   I know. Madison I don't want to be one of those crazy
             middle-aged women with a mannish haircut and a
             sensible car. I don't.

                     KANE enters.

KANE   Hi.

CAROLYN   What took you?

KANE: I wanted to have a word with David.

KANE gets a beer from the fridge.

CAROLYN: About what?

MADISON: Me.

KANE: I want you to leave the restaurant.

MADISON: Forget it.

ROYCE enters.

KANE: There are so many other places you could work.

MADISON: This isn't about me.

KANE: We need you to do this.

MADISON: It's about him.

CAROLYN: It's not.

MADISON: Why do you keep lying? You lie about when you left him—you lie about being the other woman—he lies and pretends it doesn't matter.

KANE: Everyone remembers things differently.

MADISON: Like the last time you saw him in Montreal?

CAROLYN: Montreal?

MADISON: You were there on a buying trip or something.

CAROLYN: That trip you took when I was pregnant with her?

MADISON: You ran into him.

CAROLYN: You never told me this.

KANE   It was just a coincidence.

MADISON   He never told you?

KANE   I didn't want.

CAROLYN   To make me mad?

KANE   Why are we discussing this anyway?

MADISON   Because you're all fucking liars.

ROYCE   I bet she fucked him.

CAROLYN   Royce.

ROYCE   She fucks everyone.

KANE   Don't talk about your sister like that.

ROYCE   She gets you guys crazy to cover up whatever she's got going on. Haven't you figured it out yet?

MADISON   Someone's jealous.

ROYCE   Did you fuck him?

KANE   Your sister would never do anything like that.

ROYCE   Right.

MADISON   Freak.

KANE   Would you?

MADISON   What?

KANE   Sleep with David.

MADISON   Of course not. Jeez Dad.

MADISON exits.

KANE   What is your problem?

ROYCE   I got no problems.

KANE   You had no reason to attack Madison like that.

ROYCE   I didn't attack her.

KANE   And quit being such a fucking smartass.

ROYCE   Make me.

KANE   Stop it!

CAROLYN   Kane.

ROYCE   Nice. Gonna hit me?

            Pause.

KANE   Go to bed.

            ROYCE exits.

CAROLYN   You slept with him.

KANE   No.

CAROLYN   That's why you never told me.

KANE   Nothing happened.

CAROLYN   Really?

KANE   Really.

CAROLYN   I'm going to sleep in the den tonight.

KANE   Why?

CAROLYN   I just—feel like sleeping alone.

KANE   What the fuck is going on here?

> *Lights rise on the restaurant.* DAVID's *doing bar inventory.* MADISON *is setting her cash envelope, etc. on the bar.*

MADISON   I'm outa here.

DAVID   No dinner?

MADISON   Some of the waiters are going to.

DAVID   Should we talk about the other night?

MADISON   Why are you like in love with me now or something?

DAVID   Of course not but you've been so.

MADISON   You said my father's name in my ear when you came.

DAVID   What?

MADISON   Father's name. My ear. You came.

> *Pause.*

DAVID   Maybe I was having a stroke.

MADISON   It wasn't a fucking stroke.

DAVID   Is that why are you're so angry at me?

MADISON   No I love it when the person I'm screwing thinks I'm someone else. Like my dad.

DAVID   I'm sorry. I guess you—remind me of him.

MADISON   Almost as good as the real thing?

DAVID	Don't go there.
MADISON	Why not?
DAVID	Because what happened with us has nothing to do with Kane.
MADISON	Royce knows we did it.
DAVID	What?
MADISON	He can tell. I don't know how.
DAVID	Did you admit to anything?
MADISON	Of course not.
DAVID	No one can find out.
MADISON	Why didn't you stop me?
DAVID	You were rubbing your cooch all over me.
MADISON	Dad actually asked me if I slept with you. I couldn't tell him. He would have been so hurt.
DAVID	Yes.
MADISON	And Mom.
DAVID	Oh yeah.
MADISON	I'm going to have to lie about it for the rest of my life or break their hearts.
DAVID	That's true love.
MADISON	Fuck you.

MADISON exits. Lights rise on CAROLYN scrubbing the kitchen floor. ROYCE enters. He has a black eye.

ROYCE   Don't we have a machine that does that?

CAROLYN   The floor's filthy. Jesus Royce. What happened to your
             eye?

ROYCE   Nothing.

CAROLYN   Were you in a fight?

             *CAROLYN gets a washcloth and runs it under cold
             water.*

ROYCE   I'm okay.

CAROLYN   Who did this?

ROYCE   No one.

CAROLYN   Hold this over it. Tell me what happened.

ROYCE   You guys are always telling me to stand up for myself.

CAROLYN   If you're being bullied we need to report it.

ROYCE   Some guy called me a fag and I hit him okay. He hit me
             back. Some other guys jumped in. Nothing major.

CAROLYN   Do you want to change schools again?

ROYCE   No.

             Pause.

CAROLYN   I have some good painkillers in my bathroom.

ROYCE   Mom?

CAROLYN   Yeah?

ROYCE   Why did you marry Dad if you knew he was gay?

CAROLYN   He isn't gay.

ROYCE   What is he then?

CAROLYN   Your dad.

ROYCE   You still love him though right? Nothing's changed.

              Pause.

CAROLYN   I'll get those painkillers.

              *CAROLYN exits. Lights rise on the outside of the house.
              MADISON is smoking a joint. KANE enters. She moves to
              put it out.*

MADISON   Shit Dad quit sneaking around.

KANE   Don't.

MADISON   Really?

KANE   I need a toke.

MADISON   Everyone else asleep?

KANE   I think so.

MADISON   You see Royce's eye?

KANE   I don't know whether to be worried or proud.

MADISON   Two hoots then you pass.

KANE   Sorry.

MADISON   Why did you leave David?

KANE   It was too hard.

MADISON   Being gay?

KANE   My family disowned me. My straight friends acted
             like I'd betrayed them. No one called. It was okay for
             a while. Good even. But—a party every night with the
             world's most interesting man can get very tiring.

MADISON   You must miss him sometimes.

KANE   He made me feel special.

MADISON   Yeah.

KANE   It's easy to get seduced.

MADISON   Yeah.

KANE   To do things you might not normally do.

MADISON   Yeah.

KANE   He was the best friend I'd ever had. If I hadn't met
             him. Who knows what I'd be now? Not a decorator.
             Probably not a father.

MADISON   Really?

KANE   The time I spent with David made me realize how
             important kids were to me.

MADISON   So we're here because of him?

KANE   That's not what I'm saying.

                     Pause.

MADISON   Do you still love him?

                     Long pause.

             You're supposed to say no now.

KANE   It's a—different kind of love. I don't know if it ever
            goes away. For sure you never forget it.

MADISON   Real?

KANE   Who knows?

MADISON   Why Mom?

KANE   She was so down to earth and—uncomplicated.

MADISON   Shut up.

KANE   Really. Sweet and innocent and so funny. Everything
            we said made us laugh.

MADISON   Really?

KANE   Kids only want to see their parents one way. There's a
            lot more to us you know.

MADISON   We prefer to think about ourselves.

            ROYCE enters.

ROYCE   Is that a joint?

MADISON   Yeah.

ROYCE   Gimme. Are you smoking Dad?

KANE   I had a hit or two. How's your eye?

ROYCE   Fine.

KANE   I want the names of the guys who did this.

ROYCE   Let it go.

KANE   Royce.

ROYCE   Interfere and it'll just get worse.

MADISON   Smoke.

KANE   I can't remember the last time I got high out here. I
             think Royce was a toddler.

MADISON   With Mom?

             They all laugh too loud.

KANE   Sssh.

ROYCE   Don't wanna wake her up.

MADISON   Did she ever?

KANE   Are you kidding? I used to sneak out here once in a
             blue moon when you were kids but—let's just say going
             back into the house high wasn't that much fun.

             They all laugh again.

             Stop.

ROYCE   She said she was gonna take a pill.

MADISON   Hope it was a chill pill.

ROYCE   Double dose.

MADISON   And a shot of heroin.

             They laugh.

ROYCE   Don't. It hurts.

             CAROLYN enters.

CAROLYN   Tell me you're not smoking marijuana with our
             children.

KANE   They're not really children.

MADISON   It's practically legal.

CAROLYN   Whatever happened to setting an example?

KANE   This is no different than having a drink with them.
                Anyway it's Madison's dope.

CAROLYN   Kane.

MADISON   Have a hoot Ma.

CAROLYN   Oh stop.

MADISON   It might help you get over yourself.

ROYCE   And you'll sleep like a baby.

CAROLYN   Not a chance.

KANE   We're all high anyway.

CAROLYN   I couldn't.

                MADISON holds the joint out to her.

MADISON   Betting you could.

CAROLYN   I have no idea what it's like.

ROYCE   It's nice.

                *CAROLYN takes the joint from MADISON and smokes it
                clumsily, with plenty of coughing.*

MADISON   Take little puffs.

CAROLYN   So what happens?

ROYCE   You get high.

CAROLYN   How will I know?

MADISON   Things will be—slightly different.

ROYCE   And you'll want cookies.

> *CAROLYN takes another hoot and passes the joint on.*

CAROLYN   I won't think I'm Superman and try to fly off a building or anything will I?

MADISON   That Superman pot's too expensive.

ROYCE   This stuff just makes you forget the baby in the microwave.

> *CAROLYN laughs.*

KANE   I think that story's true.

ROYCE   Yeah. Like the one about the guy with the hook.

CAROLYN   Or the lady who adopted a chihuahua that was really a rat.

MADISON   Or the hotel robber with the toothbrush in his ass on the camera.

> *They are all laughing.*

ROYCE   Or the one where the girl gets caught with the dog and the peanut butter.

CAROLYN   Or the one about the girl who meets her perfect prince and marries him and has two perfect children and they achieve if not perfection at least a normal life.

> *Their laughter grows.*

That's hysterical. The nuclear family. One day it just blows up. Ka-boom! There's a giant explosion and bingo—no more family. Everyone's become body parts in a mushroom cloud. The only thing that holds them together anymore is the fallout.

All but CAROLYN *gradually stop laughing.*

KANE   Carolyn?

ROYCE   Stop.

CAROLYN stops laughing. Pause.

CAROLYN   What's wrong?

MADISON   I'm going to bed.

CAROLYN   Aren't we having fun?

ROYCE   Total buzzkill Mom.

ROYCE and MADISON exit.

CAROLYN   What did I do?

KANE   Have you got something on your mind?

CAROLYN   No wait yes. If anything happened in Montreal everything we've had since has been a lie.

KANE   That's ridiculous.

CAROLYN   The idea of you being with him while I was pregnant. It just.

KANE   You've got to let this go.

CAROLYN   Did you marry me because you didn't want to be gay?

KANE   I married you because I wanted to spend the rest of my life with you.

Pause.

Let's go to bed.

CAROLYN   I'm gonna stay out here and stare at the stars and think about my life.

KANE   Sweetie.

CAROLYN   Don't wait up.

KANE   But.

CAROLYN   I'll probably sleep in the den again.

KANE   Right.

KANE exits.

CAROLYN   The rest of my life.

Lights rise on DAVID at the restaurant on his cellphone.

DAVID   I saw the bombing on the news. Just wanted to make sure you're okay. You're probably at work or something and I'm being silly. Call me when you get in. Really.

DAVID hangs up. MADISON enters.

MADISON   Get hold of him?

DAVID   Eleven people were killed in a city of eight million. I doubt Jefferson was one of them.

MADISON   But still. New York.

DAVID   I know.

As she speaks MADISON takes off her apron and turns in her bills and billfold.

MADISON   My section's clear.

DAVID   Still mad at me?

MADISON   Just fucked up.

DAVID   Me too.

MADISON   They're falling apart.

DAVID   Mom and Dad?

MADISON   They just seem so.

DAVID   Human?

MADISON   How do two people stay together that long?

DAVID   Insecurity codependency and fear are often the most important ingredients in a long-term relationship.

MADISON   You're too cynical. Good luck getting hold of your friend.

DAVID   Madison I'm sorry—about what happened. I should've stopped it. I know better. It's just—been so long and you're so—great.

MADISON   Like you said—I'm a grown-up now.

> *MADISON exits. DAVID takes her cash envelope and begins to exit. CAROLYN enters.*

CAROLYN   David.

DAVID   Madison just left.

CAROLYN   Good.

DAVID   You're not here to pick her up?

CAROLYN   What happened in Montreal?

DAVID   Montreal?

CAROLYN   Kane never mentioned running into you.

DAVID   Nothing important happened.

CAROLYN   I don't believe you.

DAVID   I don't care.

CAROLYN   You gave Madison a job so you can stay connected to Kane.

DAVID   I did it to piss you off Carolyn. Because you don't know anything about what Kane and I had and you have no right to qualify it.

CAROLYN   He didn't have an identity with you.

DAVID   And he does with you?

CAROLYN   Marriage takes work.

DAVID   So does denial.

CAROLYN   I know you fucked my husband in Montreal.

DAVID   You didn't think twice about fucking him when he was with me.

CAROLYN   I didn't know.

DAVID   You knew.

CAROLYN   Not for the first while. He never mentioned you and neither did anyone else. By the time he told me everything it was too late. I loved him. Trust me—I've felt guilty about it ever since.

DAVID   Good.

CAROLYN   So I'm sorry. If I took him away from you and broke
             your heart or ruined your life or whatever I'm sorry.

DAVID   You didn't take him away from me. It was already
             over. I knew how uncomfortable Kane was in our
             relationship. Never—completely there. I tried telling
             myself we could make it work but it took so much
             effort. Eventually I wanted out. I wanted to go away. I
             wanted to be gay. Really gay not pretend straight. I was
             always secretly grateful that you were there to make it
             easier for him.

CAROLYN   Oh please.

DAVID   Believe what you want.

                 Pause.

CAROLYN   When you were with him. Did he ever go away
             sometimes? In his head. Like he was dreaming about
             being somewhere else—with someone else?

DAVID   He does that with you too?

CAROLYN   Yes. I always assumed he was thinking about you.

DAVID   I assumed he was thinking about women.

CAROLYN   You didn't fuck him in Montreal?

DAVID   No.

CAROLYN   Truly?

DAVID   Whatever happened all those years ago—it doesn't
             matter now. I have no designs on your husband so why
             don't you quit pissing around and deal with whatever
             the real problem is.

CAROLYN   Excuse me?

DAVID   You started this whole thing.

CAROLYN   I did not. Madison.

DAVID   It was you who invited me to dinner Carolyn. It was you who made those ignorant gay comments that were bound to piss me off. It's you who keeps digging up the past. You.

CAROLYN   People were talking.

DAVID   If you'd just left well enough alone it would have died down when nothing happened.

CAROLYN   What are you suggesting?

DAVID   That you're using me to create drama to cover up some other inadequacy in your marriage.

CAROLYN   Oh for God's sake.

            DAVID's cellphone rings.

DAVID   Maybe you're trying to use me as an excuse for something you're afraid to do yourself.

            The cellphone rings again.

CAROLYN   Like what?

            The cellphone rings again.

DAVID   I'm sorry your hour is up. Please pay the receptionist on your way out.

CAROLYN   Goodbye.

DAVID   Bye.

CAROLYN exits. DAVID answers his phone.

Hi. Of course you're all right. Still I worry. Is it chaos? No doubt. Has anyone claimed responsibility? Terrorists are the only ones who do anymore.

Lights rise on the kitchen. KANE, ROYCE *and* MADISON *are at the table drinking coffee and looking very tired.*

MADISON   It's two nineteen.

KANE   I'm starting to get really worried.

ROYCE   Where would she go?

KANE   Maybe we should call the cops.

MADISON   She hasn't been gone long enough to call the cops.

ROYCE   Maybe she's skipped town.

MADISON   She's been strange lately.

ROYCE   Lately?

KANE   Your mother deals with a lot of different pressures. You have to give her a break once in a while.

MADISON   You're right.

CAROLYN enters.

Where the fuck have you been?

CAROLYN   Out. Driving. Thinking about a new car. I went by the old neighbourhood. Did you know the Safeway's gone?

KANE   You couldn't call?

CAROLYN   No.

KANE   Was your cell dead?

CAROLYN   No.

KANE   What's wrong?

CAROLYN   I needed some. Time. Alone.

ROYCE   Alone?

CAROLYN   To think.

                    Pause.

KANE   Did you go anywhere else?

CAROLYN   Yes.

KANE   Where?

                    Pause.

              To his restaurant?

CAROLYN   Yes.

MADISON   You saw David?

CAROLYN   Yes.

MADISON   Why?

CAROLYN   To talk.

MADISON   About what?

                    Pause.

KANE   He told you didn't he?

                    Pause.

Did he tell you?

Pause.

He fucking told you. That prick.

MADISON   What did he tell you?

Pause.

KANE   Everything. He told you everything didn't he?

Pause.

Okay we had sex. At his hotel. We did.

MADISON   I knew it.

ROYCE   Duh.

Pause.

KANE   But the other thing. It was—it wasn't real. I was just—nervous. Scared. I thought I could go back.

MADISON   Back?

KANE   There's no way I would've gone through with it. I was relieved when he said no.

ROYCE   You wanted him to take you back?

KANE   I was getting married. Going to be a father. Carolyn I was so fucking scared. I never would have went back to him for real. Never.

Long pause.

CAROLYN   He told me nothing happened. He looked me right in the eye and I bought it.

Longer pause.

KANE   Fuck.

CAROLYN   I think we should—re-evaluate our living situation.

MADISON   What does that mean?

CAROLYN   I'd like to live elsewhere for a while.

ROYCE   You can't leave. You're the mom.

CAROLYN   The mom can leave. If the kids are grown up.

ROYCE   I'm not fucking grown up.

            ROYCE exits.

MADISON   Wow.

KANE   It's the past.

CAROLYN   I should've just trusted my feelings.

KANE   It doesn't matter anymore.

CAROLYN   You're right. Good night.

KANE   Where are you sleeping?

CAROLYN   Guess.

            CAROLYN exits.

KANE   I just—I can't explain it.

            Pause.

MADISON   I understand.

MADISON exits. Lights rise on DAVID *opening a bag of clean linens and sorting them into piles. He hums to himself as he works.* ROYCE *enters holding a rifle aimed directly at* DAVID's *head.*

DAVID   You don't want to do this.

ROYCE   Wanna bet.

DAVID   It'll make everything worse.

ROYCE   Won't matter if I'm dead.

DAVID   It'll matter to your parents and sister. A lot.

ROYCE   I'm gonna kill you and then I'm going to go to the school to kill a few people there.

DAVID   It's three a.m.

ROYCE   I mean in the morning. Right after classes start. Then we'll see who's fucking laughing.

DAVID   You have a single-shot twenty-two dude. Someone'll bring you down before you reload.

ROYCE   I'll have all night to practise on your dead body.

DAVID   Someone's gonna hear the shot and call the cops.

ROYCE   I can deal with it.

DAVID   Think about your future Royce.

ROYCE   I don't have a fucking future.

DAVID   Yes you do and it'll be better.

ROYCE   Like standing up for myself was supposed to be better?

DAVID   Sure.

ROYCE *pulls his shirt up with one hand, revealing dark, painful bruises.* *

ROYCE   This is what standing up for myself got me.

DAVID   Jesus.

ROYCE   There were six of them. They wouldn't stop kicking me when I was down. This teacher finally broke it up but I could tell from the way he looked at me he didn't want to. Like I deserved it for being ugly or something.

DAVID   Put the gun down so we can talk properly.

ROYCE   No.

DAVID   Royce.

ROYCE   I'll shoot you. I mean it.

                   Pause.

DAVID   I can give you a job.

ROYCE   Too late.

DAVID   Do you want me to fuck you?

ROYCE   Sex is gross.

DAVID   Everyone has sexual feelings.

ROYCE   I don't. I've been looking at porn since I was eight years old and it's the most repulsive thing I've ever seen.

DAVID   Then why are you looking at it?

ROYCE   Hoping something'll kick in. Everyone's fucking hooked on it. Guys at school have hardcore porn on their iPods—their cellphones. I know girls in the tenth grade who run fuck sites out of their bedrooms. Sigfreid's got this sick shit you wouldn't believe. I had to threaten to tell his parents about it to get the gun.

DAVID   Real sex isn't like porn.

ROYCE   I know. That weird fucking sound my dad makes. And her. You'd never hear that in a movie.

DAVID   Sex makes people do stupid things.

ROYCE   Y'think?

DAVID   Look at your parents. At me. But you don't have this stupid weakness. You won't make those same mistakes. You're actually lucky.

ROYCE   Don't try getting all confidential with me like you understand Mr. Perfect Teeth Mr. Wonderful Hair.

DAVID   It's a weave.

ROYCE   What?

DAVID   Everything above my ears is a careful fake attached to my own thinning hair by invisible microfibres.

ROYCE   Get out.

DAVID   Check for yourself.

ROYCE   You'll just try to grab the gun.

DAVID   No look. I'll put my hands behind my back. Just feel.

          ROYCE *touches the top of* DAVID's *head.*

          See.

ROYCE   Weird. Like Astroturf.

DAVID	My smile?
ROYCE	Yeah.
DAVID	Forty thousand dollars.
ROYCE	Shut up.
DAVID	Not a single filling. Who do you know that doesn't have a single filling? And this waistline.
ROYCE	Yeah?
DAVID	Three inches removed with liposuction. Five grand.
ROYCE	No way.
DAVID	If you look just at the bottom of my eyebrows you can see very faint scars from the eye lift. Seven large. I also spend four days a week at the gym working out for at least two hours. I eat plain chicken breast raw vegetables and rice cakes for most of the week and I just fucking hate it.
ROYCE	Then why do you do it?
DAVID	Because I don't want to be discarded. I don't want to be not sexy. Not viable. Not yet. See. It makes us all do crazy things and you're blessed if you seriously aren't interested.
ROYCE	Quit talking.
DAVID	Am I making too much sense?
ROYCE	You're pissing me off.
DAVID	Royce if you were going to shoot me you would have done it by now.

Pause.

Put the gun down. We can talk.

Pause.

ROYCE   Are you going to call the cops?

DAVID   Not if you give me the rifle.

ROYCE   You can't tell my parents.

DAVID   We'll work something out.

ROYCE   Work something out?

DAVID   Give me the gun.

> *ROYCE hands DAVID the rifle.*

ROYCE   Mom's leaving.

DAVID   Why?

ROYCE   Because of Montreal. I don't.

> *DAVID suddenly hits ROYCE with the butt of the gun,
> very hard on the bruised area. ROYCE screams in pain.*

Ow! Fuck! What did you do that for?

DAVID   That's the first bullet hitting a Mormon girl you don't
even know.

ROYCE   What?! Shit.

> *DAVID hits ROYCE again in the bruised area. ROYCE
> screams.*

DAVID   That's the second bullet hitting a Chinese kid from
your English class.

ROYCE   Okay! I get it!

DAVID   This isn't a fucking game. People get hurt. Really hurt.
           And it's never the bullies who get it.

           DAVID hits ROYCE.

ROYCE   Don't hurt me anymore!

DAVID   Get up.

ROYCE   Don't hurt me. Please don't hurt me anymore. Please
           don't. Please.

           *DAVID sets the rifle on the table and kneels down to help
           ROYCE up. ROYCE throws his arms around DAVID and
           sobs. DAVID holds ROYCE and soothes him. Lights rise on
           CAROLYN passing through the kitchen with extra linen.
           KANE is opening a beer.*

KANE   Marriages go through phases.

CAROLYN   This isn't a phase.

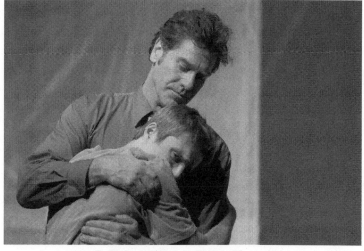

From the production at Factory Theatre.
David Keeley as David and Andrew Craig as Royce.
Photograph by Ed Gass-Donnelly.

KANE   It is. It's part of marriage. Right now we don't like each
                other very much.

CAROLYN   You don't like me?

KANE   Of course I do. I love you. But when you're acting like
                this. Look we knew when we decided to commit that
                there were going to be bad times. But we swore we
                weren't going to be like other parents and throw in the
                towel or establish a bloodless partnership for the sake
                of appearances. Sure there have been occasional times
                when I've hated you or was repulsed by the thought
                of touching you—and I know you've felt the same
                way about me. But we're a team Carolyn. We built
                this house as a team we run our business as a team we
                raised our kids as a team.

CAROLYN   I know.

KANE   That's a pretty big accomplishment to toss away.

CAROLYN   I'm not tossing it away. I'm just—thinking about
                moving on to some other accomplishment.

KANE   Please don't say that.

CAROLYN   What if David had said yes? Taken you back.

KANE   He didn't.

CAROLYN   You'd be living with him and I'd be raising Madison on
                my own.

                KANE moves to CAROLYN and puts his arms around her.

KANE   I get drunk on the way you smell. My dick gets chubby
                at the sound of your voice. I can't imagine sleeping
                without your body next to mine. I've never loved
                anyone the way I love you.

CAROLYN has gotten turned on. She tries to get away from him.

CAROLYN   Kane please.

KANE   What?

CAROLYN   Don't you see.

KANE   You can't walk away from the business.

CAROLYN   The way this all happened. Madison moving out. Royce finishing high school. David coming back. The timing is right.

KANE   The timing couldn't be worse.

CAROLYN breaks away from KANE.

CAROLYN   I meant it's right for me.

KANE   Carolyn don't leave I can't I don't I have a belly. I'm old and I have a belly.

CAROLYN   Kane.

CAROLYN moves to KANE and kisses him softly.

KANE   Don't stop loving me.

CAROLYN   I never will.

KANE   Please.

CAROLYN   But I've never had another lover. Or been through a breakup or lived on my own.

They're kissing one another softly. Both are crying.

KANE   It's not as good as you think.

CAROLYN   Woke up alone. Called a girlfriend up for coffee.

KANE   It's not worth losing your family over.

> *Their hands begin to move over each other's bodies sensually.*

CAROLYN   I'm just renegotiating the terms of engagement.

KANE   I can't wake up without you.

CAROLYN   We shouldn't.

KANE   It's always so good.

CAROLYN   Yeah but.

> *They have started to fuck.*

KANE   Please don't leave me.

CAROLYN   I have to.

From the production at Factory Theatre.
Julie Stewart as Carolyn and Ashley Wright as Kane.
Photograph by Ed Gass-Donnelly.

KANE   I love you so much.

CAROLYN   I love you.

              They fuck. Lights rise on the empty kitchen. The door
              opens very carefully. DAVID *and* ROYCE *enter.* DAVID *is*
              carrying the rifle and supporting ROYCE *with the other*
              arm.

ROYCE   Ssh.

              DAVID *deposits* ROYCE *in a chair.*

DAVID   Here's the deal. I take the rifle back to Sigfreid's and
              no one knows what happened. But if you renege on
              what we talked about I wake your parents up right now
              and tell them everything.

ROYCE   Don't make me.

DAVID   No negotiation.

ROYCE   They'll hate me.

DAVID   Do it or I will.

              Pause.

              Royce.

ROYCE   Okay shut up.

DAVID   Remember you keep my secrets and I keep yours.

ROYCE   Mom! Dad! I need to talk to you right now!

              DAVID *opens the door.*

DAVID   Again.

ROYCE   I need to talk to you!

KANE   *(off)* Hello?

CAROLYN   *(off)* Royce?

> *KANE and CAROLYN are heard approaching offstage. DAVID winks at ROYCE.*

DAVID   Tell them.

ROYCE   Alright.

> *DAVID exits, closing the door quietly behind him. CAROLYN enters pulling her robe on.*

CAROLYN   Royce?

> *KANE enters doing up his pants and pulling his undershirt on.*

KANE   Son?

> *Pause.*

ROYCE   I need help.

CAROLYN   What?

ROYCE   Please.

KANE   What can we do?

ROYCE   Please help me. Please someone help me. I'm really really sad all the time and I need someone to help me. Please. Help me.

> *Lights rise on DAVID at the restaurant. He's checking the glassware for spots. MADISON enters.*

DAVID   Everything okay?

MADISON   Sure. Where am I?

DAVID	Six. And there's only one busboy for the entire house tonight.
MADISON	That blows.
DAVID	Labour and food costs are too high and reservations are too low. How are things at home?

Pause.

Madison?

MADISON	Royce had some kind of—breakdown. They're doing tests in the hospital. He's like totally bipolar or something. He's—so sad.
DAVID	The doctors will help him be less sad.
MADISON	That's not the same as happy.
DAVID	It's a start.
MADISON	Mom's moving out—but not till the Royce thing's resolved.
DAVID	What's your dad doing through all this?
MADISON	Drinking a lot of beer smoking like a chimney and living at the office.
DAVID	Great.
MADISON	I want to tell them. What we did.
DAVID	Absolutely not.
MADISON	The truth makes things better.
DAVID	This isn't about the truth. This is about getting back at your parents and making them responsible for our bad decision.

MADISON   Why would I want to hurt them?

DAVID   It takes the spotlight off of Royce and puts it back on you.

MADISON   Fuck you.

DAVID   Time to grow up.

MADISON   I still think I should.

DAVID   Don't do it Madison. I mean it.

MADISON   Are you threatening me?

DAVID   Yes.

MADISON   But I feel so guilty.

DAVID   That's how we adults remember our mistakes. Now get set up. We open in fifteen minutes.

MADISON   You're an asshole.

DAVID   I know. Now do your fucking job.

> *Lights rise on* CAROLYN *in a hospital room with* ROYCE.

CAROLYN   The doctor says you're doing quite well.

ROYCE   Yeah.

CAROLYN   The talks with the therapist?

ROYCE   Okay.

CAROLYN   The pills?

ROYCE   Helping.

CAROLYN   You're not having compulsive suicidal thoughts are you? We're supposed to watch for that.

ROYCE   No.

CAROLYN   They said something about possible—sexual side effects.

ROYCE   I'm asexual Mom.

CAROLYN   Is that—official now?

ROYCE   Yes.

CAROLYN   We accept you for who you are.

ROYCE   The doctor suggested some websites and support groups.

CAROLYN   I'm sure you'll find them very helpful.

ROYCE   They're for you and Dad.

CAROLYN   Right of course. Do you feel like you might want to come home soon?

ROYCE   Are you still sleeping in the den?

CAROLYN   It doesn't matter where I'm sleeping as long as we're all together.

ROYCE   I miss those horrible sounds you guys made when you got it on.

CAROLYN   Stop.

ROYCE   Can't you?

CAROLYN   I don't think I can.

ROYCE   Why not?

CAROLYN   My feelings have—changed.

ROYCE   Love can't just go away.

CAROLYN   No but it does become—other things. Other kinds of love.

ROYCE   And this is all because of the Montreal thing?

CAROLYN   No.

ROYCE   Does every marriage fail?

CAROLYN   No but a lot of them expire.

ROYCE   Then why get married?

CAROLYN   When you fall in love with someone you have to believe it's forever. It's not real otherwise.

ROYCE   Are you on medication?

CAROLYN   Just half a lorazepam before I came in. My doctor prescribed them. They help a lot. Anyway love—you know—that one word doesn't really do the job of describing how mixed-up those feelings really are. My feelings for your father have changed. I don't love him the way I used to but I do still love him.

ROYCE   But not enough to stay.

CAROLYN   Right.

ROYCE   Thanks.

CAROLYN   For what?

ROYCE   Not lying to me.

CAROLYN   Come home Royce. You're ready

ROYCE   Okay.

                    KANE enters.

KANE   Things at the school took longer than expected.

CAROLYN   And?

KANE   And I've got all of your assignments for the rest of the term so you never have to go back there again.

ROYCE   Thanks Pop.

CAROLYN   Royce is ready to come home.

KANE   You're sure?

ROYCE   Yeah. This place is boring.

KANE   Alright.

ROYCE   They want me to come in every other day for a while — I start group therapy next week — and I have to stay on the meds.

CAROLYN   Of course.

ROYCE   They want me to do some sessions with you guys too.

KANE   Of course. Royce. We.

ROYCE   Yeah.

KANE   We love you.

CAROLYN   More than anything in life.

ROYCE   Even if I'm crazy.

KANE   You're not crazy.

ROYCE   But I'm.

CAROLYN   Recovering. You're recovering.

KANE   Let's go.

            Lights rise on DAVID *at the restaurant checking cash
            envelopes.* MADISON *enters with her envelope.*

MADISON   One of the chairs is off-kilter at five C.

DAVID   I'll get it fixed. How's Royce?

MADISON   He's started talking to me again. For real. He told me
            about the gun thing. Thank you.

DAVID   It was a cry for help.

MADISON   But pretty fucked up.

DAVID   He's getting what he needs now.

MADISON   You were right about telling my parents too. It would
            have made everything worse. I just—secrets have a
            way of getting out.

DAVID   Not when it's shared by only two people. A secret's not
            the same as a lie. There's cassoulet left over. Are you
            hungry?

MADISON   Yeah but well no—I told some of the guys I'd meet
            them in a few minutes.

DAVID   Is Willett going?

MADISON   He'll probably be there.

DAVID   He makes you laugh.

MADISON   Yeah.

DAVID   Not too hard on the eyes either.

MADISON   Okay now you're starting to sound jealous.

DAVID   I'd gotten used to—having someone to eat with.

MADISON   We'll eat again.

DAVID   But not like we used to.

From the production at the Royal Exchange Theatre.
Jonny Phillips as David.
Photograph by Jonathan Keenan.

MADISON   No and that's totally my fault. I just have this thing where I have to fuck every guy I meet. I need to work on it and I will really. But right now I gotta.

DAVID   Don't worry. Good night.

           MADISON exits. DAVID goes to the kitchen briefly and returns with a bowl of food, a glass and a carafe of wine. He pours himself a large glass of wine and sits down to eat alone. Lights rise on the kitchen of the Sawatsky house, empty. MADISON enters dressed entirely in black. She moves to a counter, pulls out a bottle of vodka and pours a slug into a glass. She downs the shot and pours more. ROYCE enters, also in black. He shares a look with MADISON, reaches into his pocket and takes out a pill bottle. He takes a pill using what's left of MADISON's vodka to wash it down.

MADISON   Those help?

ROYCE   It's like being wrapped in something cloudy.

MADISON   But you don't feel as down.

ROYCE   I don't feel as anything.

MADISON   Great.

           KANE enters dressed entirely in black.

           Shot?

KANE   Set me up.

           MADISON pours a shot into a glass and hands it to KANE. KANE downs the shot and holds the glass out to MADISON. She pours another shot into it.

MADISON   Funerals are vile traditions.

KANE   They help with closure.

CAROLYN enters dressed in black.

CAROLYN   Closure's overrated.

MADISON waves the bottle at her mother.

MADISON   Takes the edge off.

CAROLYN   Okay.

MADISON pours her mother a shot. KANE raises his glass.

KANE   To Herbert Carver.

CAROLYN   It was nice of so many of his former students to show
            up.

MADISON   They were so old.

CAROLYN   He loved to read. It was like a religion to him. He
            picked a book for each year of my childhood and read
            it to me until I was old enough to read myself. Then he
            gave me a book for every birthday until he—got sick.
            It was how we communicated.

MADISON   Who besides me needs another drink?

ROYCE   There's something I should probably tell you guys.

            Pause.

CAROLYN   Well?

ROYCE   I've met someone. Special.

KANE   Someone?

CAROLYN   Special? But I thought you were.

ROYCE   I am.

KANE   And is she he?

ROYCE   She. Her uncle raped her repeatedly between the ages
            of two and seven so she hates sex. She's the sister of
            this guy I know from group. Her name's Tasha. She's
            not very pretty but she's really smart. And funny.

            Pause.

CAROLYN   Good for you.

ROYCE   We share feelings of inadequacy and internalized
            self-hatred.

KANE   It's important to have things in common.

ROYCE   And our med cycles are simpatico.

MADISON   Great.

ROYCE   The doctor says it's a sign of progress.

MADISON   I have an announcement of my own.

CAROLYN   What's that?

MADISON   Willett and I are going to try monogamy.

            Pause.

KANE   Who the hell's Willett?

MADISON   My boyfriend.

CAROLYN   Boyfriend?

MADISON   I've been seeing him for nearly two months.

CAROLYN   Is he—nice?

MADISON   He thinks he's far smarter and better looking than he
            actually is but I really kinda like him.

ROYCE   And he's a waiter?

MADISON   Just part-time while he goes to university.

CAROLYN   Great. What's he taking?

MADISON   Political science don't even get me started. If the
            relationship lasts another two months I'll introduce
            you.

CAROLYN   I found an apartment.

            Pause.

            It's just a few blocks away. Walking distance.

            Pause.

            I also found a job. I'm going to be doing the books for
            a trucking company.

MADISON   Trucking company?

ROYCE   Whoa.

CAROLYN   I liked the women in their bookkeeping office.

            MADISON pours KANE a shot. He downs it.

ROYCE   I guess if it'll make you happier.

MADISON   Right.

CAROLYN   There are two extra bedrooms. You kids can stay
            whenever you want.

ROYCE   Great.

MADISON   I wouldn't be very comfortable sleeping there.

CAROLYN   You'll get used to it eventually.

MADISON   I hate it when you say things like that.

CAROLYN   That's why I say them.

MADISON   I know.

KANE   Well okay then now.

                    Pause.

MADISON   I'm meeting Willett.

KANE   Don't be too late.

                    MADISON kisses KANE.

MADISON   Don't wait up.

CAROLYN   Please don't hate me forever.

MADISON   Working on it.

                    MADISON exits.

ROYCE   I'm tired and my mouth is really dry.

CAROLYN   Good night sweetie. We'll talk tomorrow.

                    ROYCE exits.

KANE   It's not going to be as great as you think.

CAROLYN   Whatever it was we were meant to do together—it's
             done. It is. You know it too. It's all just habit now. Fear
             of the unknown.

KANE   But I love you.

CAROLYN   I know.

             Pause.

             Don't forget to replace the furnace.

KANE   Right.

             *CAROLYN exits. KANE goes to the fridge and gets himself
             a beer. He sits at the table and sips the beer. Lights rise on
             DAVID in the restaurant. He's looking at the reservation
             book and shaking his head. MADISON enters.*

MADISON   What's going on?

DAVID   What?

MADISON   You haven't looked me in the eye for the last two days.

DAVID   Let's talk after your shift.

MADISON   I'd rather talk now.

DAVID   After your shift is better. Really.

MADISON   You're going to fire me.

DAVID   Yes.

MADISON   Why?

DAVID   My costs are through the roof and with this
             downswing.

MADISON   Why me?

DAVID   Last hired first fired.

MADISON   That's me and Willett.

DAVID   And three of the kitchen staff and one dishwasher.

MADISON   This is about him isn't it?

DAVID   No.

MADISON   I see you watching us all the time.

DAVID   I watch you and Willett because I can see you falling in love and it's such a wonderful thing I can't not look.

MADISON   Seriously?

DAVID   I don't think Willett's the sharpest knife in the drawer and thankfully I doubt he's going to be your one great love but I know you're enjoying it and that makes me feel—surprisingly good.

MADISON   But you still have to fire me.

DAVID   Yes. You won't have any trouble finding another job. You should be someplace where you can make real money anyway.

MADISON   True. Think Mary'll close the place?

DAVID   Hopefully not—if we can get our budgets in line. I'll probably pick up some floor shifts.

MADISON   Waiting? Really?

            DAVID nods.

            That's sad.

DAVID   Anything necessary to survive. You don't have to work your shift if.

MADISON   Don't worry. I'll do it.

DAVID   You're sure?

            MADISON moves to DAVID and gives him a quick kiss.

MADISON   Thank you.

>   *DAVID kisses her again.*

DAVID   No thank you.

>   *They hug.*

             Dinner later?

>   *Short pause.*

MADISON   You know it.

>   *MADISON exits. Lights rise on CAROLYN at her new place.*
>   *She's getting ready to go out. There's a knock at the door*
>   *and ROYCE enters using his key.*

CAROLYN   Hey handsome.

ROYCE   That your new car in the lot?

CAROLYN   Like it?

ROYCE   It's kinda showy.

CAROLYN   That's the point.

ROYCE   I like it. Tasha and I are on our way to the cat show. You
             wanna come?

CAROLYN   That's so sweet. Where is Tasha?

ROYCE   Didn't want to come in because she saw one of her
             dead guys sitting on your steps.

CAROLYN   Thanks but I already have plans.

ROYCE   Like a date?

CAROLYN   Like drinks with some of the girls from work.

ROYCE   Sounds fun.

CAROLYN   Thanks beats sitting alone in front of the TV for
             another night. How's Kane?

ROYCE   Don't ask.

CAROLYN   Try to get him out of the house.

ROYCE   We're working on it. Have fun.

CAROLYN   You too.

             *ROYCE blows CAROLYN a kiss then exits. Lights rise on
             the restaurant. DAVID is carrying two plates of food to a
             table. KANE enters.*

DAVID   She's just finishing up. This is her last night.

KANE   You finally fired her?

DAVID   Business is shit.

KANE   Sorry to hear that.

DAVID   But not sorry to see her go.

KANE   It doesn't really matter anymore.

DAVID   She won't have a problem finding another job. She's
             very good. Hold on. I'll get her.

             *DAVID gestures for KANE to sit at the table and exits.
             KANE is tempted by the wonderful smell of the pasta.
             He dips his finger into the sauce on one plate and tastes
             it. It's amazing. DAVID enters with MADISON's apron,
             billfold, cash envelope, etc.*

             Apparently she finished her section early and slipped
             out the back door.

KANE   She phoned me for a ride half an hour ago.

DAVID   Debra saw her drive away with Willett.

KANE   Then why would she need a ride?

DAVID   She knew I was making a final dinner.

            Short pause.

            Oh.

KANE   Oh.

DAVID   Yes.

KANE   Set-up and everything.

DAVID   She mentioned you weren't getting out much.

KANE   She says you never go anywhere.

DAVID   She's wrong. I go to lots of places. Just no place fun.

KANE   What is this?

DAVID   Three-cheese tortellini in an aromatic tomato vodka sauce.

KANE   Smells amazing.

DAVID   Hungry?

KANE   I've been eating out of the microwave for months.

DAVID   Would you like to join me?

KANE   You wouldn't mind?

            Short pause.

DAVID   No.

KANE   Okay.

DAVID   Wine?

KANE   Please.

            DAVID pours wine for them both.

DAVID   How you doing?

KANE   My family's fallen apart. You?

DAVID   My restaurant's failing and I have no life or friends.

            Pause.

KANE   I am such a total failure.

DAVID   No.

KANE   My wife—my kids are—

DAVID   Fucked up. Who isn't? They're essentially good people—and interesting. That's more than a lot of parents accomplish.

KANE   Since Carolyn left me. I can't. It's. Just.

            Pause.

DAVID   Have some wine.

KANE   Thanks. Sorry. Can I smoke in here?

DAVID   No.

KANE   I've been very—emotional lately.

DAVID   Perfectly understandable.

KANE   I bet you feel like you know my family almost as well as
          I do.

DAVID   Almost.

          Pause.

KANE   I still don't understand any of this.

DAVID   Shit happens. We never really know why.

KANE   It's been a long time.

DAVID   Doesn't seem like it.

KANE   I guess there's a lot we can catch up on.

DAVID   Yeah. And we will. Later.

KANE   You're sure? That might be kinda weird after
          everything.

DAVID   Kane.

KANE   What?

DAVID   Eat.

          They eat as the lights slowly fade to black.

SPECIAL THANKS AND ACKNOWLEDGEMENTS
Iris Turcott, Tamara Bernier-Evans, Trina Davies, Peni Christopher, BJ Radomski, Ken Gass, Brent Carver, Noah Reid, Arin Mackinnon, Michael Spencer-Davis and, as always, my greatest supporter and collaborator, Braham Murray and the wonderful people at the Royal Exchange Theatre.

photo by Manon Cousin

Brad Fraser is a playwright, director and producer whose work has been greeted with success across the globe, garnering him such awards as the London Evening Standard Award for most promising playwright, the LA Critics Award and Toronto's Dora Mavor Moore Award for best new play to name only a few. His films include *Love and Human Remains* (directed by Academy Award-winner Denys Arcand and winner of the Genie Award for Best Adapted Screenplay) and *Leaving Metropolis*, adapted from *Poor Super Man*. For television, he spent three seasons as a writer/producer on *Queer As Folk* for Showtime and two seasons hosting his chat show *Jawbreaker with Brad Fraser* on OutTV. Check out Bradfraser.net for more info and occasional updates.